D1547141

791.1 Gr — $9.95

Gryczan, Matthew
Carnival secrets

DATE DUE

DE 26 '90			
JA 26 '91			
NO 2 '91			
FE 7 '92			
AG 19 '92			
MAY 17 '94			
OCT 05 '94			
AG 24 '01			
SE 17 '05			

EAU CLAIRE DISTRICT LIBRARY

DEMCO

Carnival Secrets

How to Win at Carnival Games

Which Games to Avoid

How to Make Your Own Games

By Matthew Gryczan

First edition – Zenith Press

4/11/90 B&T $9.95

EAU CLAIRE DISTRICT LIBRARY

74022

Carnival Secrets

How to Win at Carnival Games

By Matthew Gryczan

Published by:
Zenith Press, P.O. Box 248, Royal Oak, Mich. 48068

All rights reserved. No part of this book may be reproduced or transmitted in any form or by any means, electronic or mechanical, including photocopying, recording, or any information storage and retrieval system without written permission from the author, except for the inclusion of brief quotations in a review.

Copyright ©1988 by Matthew L. Gryczan.
First Printing 1988.
Printed in the United States of America.
ISBN 0-945974-00-0.
Library of Congress Catalog Card Number 88-50094.

To my wife Ann, for her unwavering patience while this book was being written.

Warning – Disclaimer

Photos of games and carnival operators appearing in this book were included strictly to illustrate how the games are played. It was not the author's intention to illustrate the operation of an illegal game or an operator who cheated, and in no case in this book is there a photo of an operator who ran a rigged game.

Parts of this book describe how some carnival games can be rigged, but the reader should not assume that all games on a midway are run unfairly. By and large, carnival games are run honestly. This book serves only as a guide to better educate the public on how some games can be gaffed.

Although the information contained in this book was researched as thoroughly as possible, there may be mistakes in content. While all pages were proofread under normal publishing standards, there may be mistakes in typography. The author does not assume any liability resulting from mistakes in either content or typography.

This book was written as a general guide, with the purpose of educating and entertaining the public with regard to carnival games. Neither the author nor Zenith Press shall assume liability with respect to any loss or damage caused or alleged to be caused directly or indirectly through the use of this book.

Table of Contents

Acknowledgments

In writing this book, the author drew on the experiences of many people and studies conducted by local, state and federal agencies. It would be impractical to list all the sources here.

But special thanks for help in preparing this book go to William Riedthaler, special deputy with the Cuyahoga County Sheriff's Office in Cleveland; Tom Dawson, chairman of Acme Premium Supply Corp. in St. Louis; Bob Snyder, president of Bob Snyder & Associates, Walnut, Calif.; Terry Hampton, president of Hampton Co. Inc. in Burlington, Mich.; William Holmes, agent with the gambling unit of the FBI laboratory; R.K. Larson, executive director of the Outdoor Amusement Business Assn. Inc. in Minneapolis; Jim Hatchett, owner of the J.A. Hatchett Mfg. Co. in Rolla, Mo.; Dwain Dennis, detective with the Ionia County Sheriff Department, Ionia, Mich.; John Mulvaney, with the Michigan attorney general's office; James Story, detective with the Oklahoma City Police Department; The University of Regina, Regina, Saskatchewan; The Kansas Bureau of Investigation; Chuck Schofield, lieutenant with the Peoria County Sheriff's Department, Peoria County, Ill.; June Hardin, president of Wapello Fabrications Inc., Wapello, Iowa, and John Mendes Jr., general manager of Bob's Space Racers Inc., Daytona Beach, Fla.

Edited by Betty Lou Kitzman
Diagrams by the author and Rhonda Rudnick
Photos, except where noted, by the author

About the Author

Matthew Gryczan collected information and conducted interviews of carnival game manufacturers, law enforcement agents and carnies for two years in preparation of Carnival Secrets. He also measured games as they operated on the midway and kept track of how many times the average carnivalgoer had to play before winning. He then built replicas of some games and practiced them.

The outcome of his research: He won 10 large prizes the first year he hit the carnival circuit, spending far less per game than the average player.

Gryczan, managing editor of a Detroit business publication, has worked as an editor of two magazines and a reporter on four daily newspapers over the past 10 years. He holds bachelor's degrees in journalism and business.

Chapter 1

Behind the Scenes

This book was written for those who watch with envy as someone struts along a carnival midway with a large stuffed animal, and ask themselves: "How did he or she win?"

The author put that question to carnival patrons, carnies, manufacturers of carnival games and law enforcement agents. Responses ran the gamut depending on who was answering – from police who said it was sheer luck to carnies who said it was largely skill.

Needless to say, the police and the carnies both said the other was all wrong.

Conflicting opinion is a rule of the midways. So, what is contained in this book is the hardest evidence available on the best way to win at carnival games. The information was collected through direct observation and measurement, photographs and personal interviews. Hearsay and unsubstantiated opinion were kept to a minimum.

More than 40 games are outlined in this book, along with explanations of how they are played, how to build and practice some of the games, the odds of winning some of the games, and the most common methods of gaffing them.

Which games should people play, and how can they win? That depends on the game itself and on the operator or agent who runs the game.

Two Latin words describe how a player should approach carnival games: *caveat emptor*, meaning "Let the buyer beware."

Some games are out-and-out frauds that players can never win.

Avoid these games, and advise others to do so, too. The carnival industry will improve its reputation greatly when every last operator of Razzle Dazzle, Over the Rail, Scissor Bucket, Swinger and other such scams has been run off the midway.

Most games fall into a gray area: They can be run honestly, or they can be "worked strong" – in other words, operated so the player has little chance of winning. Carnies and police agree that there is a way to cheat at every game on the midway. Most games are run on the up-and-up, but some aren't. Don't assume that your local police department can protect you against grifters or flatties – carny names for operators who cheat the public. Learn all you can about your favorite games, and reward honest operators by playing their games. Penalize shady operators by avoiding their "flat stores."

The first tip-off that a game is gaffed is the prize offered. Never, under any circumstances, play for money, unless you are in an area where gambling is legal, such as Nevada or Atlantic City. The offer of an illegal wager is the surest sign that a game is rigged.

And players are naive to compete for expensive prizes such as color television sets or gold jewelry. They aren't dealing with an operator who has a large stock of goods, such as a local appliance store, and happily turns over a $200 TV set for $5. No one wins those large, expensive prizes displayed in the carny's booth. Police report that many people have lost thousands of dollars on such operations.

Carnies freely admit that they can control the number of prizes, or stock, they give out by making a game easier or harder to win. A carny does this by moving a target back a foot, spreading glass plates farther apart, changing the angle on a backboard, etc. Within reason, this isn't cheating.

The rule of thumb to apply is this: You probably have a fair chance of winning a game if the carny can successfully demonstrate how to win and you get to use the same equipment and stand where the carny stood while playing.

A perfect example of this is Cover the Spot, a game in which the player must cover a large red circle with five round metal plates. Carnies spend hours practicing this game until they make it look easy to win; and many of them will say outright that it is a difficult game.

Law enforcement agents complain that Cover the Spot is too hard for the average person to win. But the author doesn't think that opinion is fair to the carny. The game requires practice, but those who either spend the money to learn on the midway or practice with a homemade set will be rewarded by winning. The author won Cover the Spot at several carnivals after he built a replica of the game and practiced at home.

Now, some would say Cover the Spot isn't fair because not many people will take the trouble to build a game and practice it for several hours. The author's rejoinder is: Players don't deserve to win if they don't practice. Running a carnival game is a business, and carnies can't afford to give away large prizes for games everyone can easily win.

There are a good number of games like Cover the Spot on the midway that are honestly run but require practice to win. This book includes plans on how to build Cover the Spot, Whiffle Ball and other games, so you can practice before the next carnival reaches your town.

Group games and percentage games generally are fair. Group games that rely on skill, such as Kentucky Derby and Water Race, generally are run honestly because the carny doesn't have to cheat to make a decent profit. There is only one winner, and people essentially are playing against each other rather than the operator. The carny varies the size of the prize with the size of the group playing, so the profit remains roughly the same.

Percentage games that rely on chance, such as Crazy Ball, generally are fair, and they probably offer the person who has little athletic skill the best chance to win a large prize at a carnival. However, those kinds of games may be outlawed in some cities because they are games of chance.

Athletic games such as Ladder Climb, Skee-Ball and Roller Bowler are fair, but that isn't synonymous with easy-to-win. In this book, the reader will learn what manufacturers say are the secrets to winning these games, and will be given rough estimates on the odds of a person winning.

Hanky panks – games operated so players are assured of walking away with some sort of cheap souvenir, nicknamed "slum" or "plaster" – usually are honestly run. Hanky panks generally award prizes worth less than the cost per play, and make their profit because of the large volume of customers. Duck Pond, Guess Your Weight and Age, and Pitch-Till-You-Win are examples of this family of games.

To win the larger prizes, players should concentrate on one or two games they can excel at when they visit a midway.

Carnies and law enforcement agents agree that any game on the midway can be gaffed by an operator so players will lose. Consequently, the chance of winning also depends on the operator of the game.

There is a rich variety of individuals running games on the midway. Many run their games squarely, but a few attempt to take the player for every nickel they can get. A carnivalgoer might run into Marie, a carny for more than 20 years, who earns money from the midway to pay property taxes and buy a few luxuries with her husband . . . or T.J., a 25-year-old carny who wants desperately to start his own concession but can't because he lives under several aliases and hasn't paid income taxes for six years.

By and large, carnies are small-business operators not unlike the shop owners found in every city and town in the United States. They have families, dream of retirement, pay taxes and work long, hard hours for several months of the year. For many of them, carnival life is a heritage. Almost every carny interviewed for this book said he or she was born into the carnival life, and several had children who already were working on the midway.

As in any other business, operators of carnival games must make a profit. They do this essentially in two ways: by charging more to play a game than the prizes cost and letting virtually everyone win; or by awarding prizes worth more than the cost of a play and wagering that only a small percentage will win.

Ask carnies about your chances of winning at their booths, or joints, and they will give you a puzzled look. They'll think a bit, then say: "Oh, I throw about 25 percent stock." Now it's your turn to look puzzled.

Carnies generally don't think in terms of odds and probabilities. They think in terms of throwing stock: How much of the gross revenues is given back to carnivalgoers in the form of prizes.

The player can get a feel for his or her odds in the game by looking at the prizes and the cost of the game per play.

Let's see what a carny means by "throwing 25 percent stock." Let's say a wholesaler is offering some good-looking plush – a term for stuffed animals – at $1.50 a unit. The carny first judges whether the prize will attract a good tip: a group of players and prospective players. The more attractive the plush, the more profit he or she can make.

The carny decides he or she wants to charge $1 per play and will throw 25 percent stock, a fairly normal percentage for a midway game. This means that 25 cents of every dollar taken in goes to pay for the prize. So, in this case, the carny figures he or she should be awarding a prize in one out of six plays – $1.50 divided by 25 cents.

The carny then selects a game that he or she has learned, through trial and error, awards that many prizes per number of plays.

Carnies protect themselves from knowledgeable players whose skills exceed those of the average player by posting a sign stating that only one prize is awarded per day per person.

Where does the other 75 cents of the player's dollar go? There are a number of other expenses involved in running the joint, such as electricity, utilities hookup, labor, transportation, storage of goods, and privilege – rent paid to the carnival owner to operate on the midway. And there is profit, the reason why the carny – or any small-business person – is working in the first place.

Don't expect a carny to throw 50 percent stock – in effect, give 50-50 odds on playing a game. They have to make money to cover their expenses, and they would go out of business if they paid such a high percentage.

Carnivalgoers may not realize that running a carnival game is a risky business, as uncertain as trying to predict what the weather will be on a particular day six months from now. With all apologies to Poor Richard and his almanac, no one knows when rain will cut attendance at an outdoor carnival.

Carnival work also is a seasonal business. The carnival season is generally late April to early October, and carnies make the bulk of their income, if not their whole livelihood, in that six-month period.

On top of that, a carnival game is not your local store. A person who walks into a store to buy an item knows exactly what the price will be, and so does the shopkeeper. The shopkeeper has a much easier time calculating profits and expenses than a carny does.

On the midway, the carny and the player generally are competing – one betting against the other's skills. This adds to the excitement and satisfaction of winning a carnival game, and that amusement value is hard to quantify.

To be fair to local shops, carnival games generally don't offer the necessities of daily life. Only a few people would visit a store and buy a large stuffed animal. A good number of the stuffed animals awarded on the midway are big on flash – the outward appearance that draws players to a game – and small on quality. Many animals are stuffed with fiberfill or cellulose, a filling inferior to that found in a high-quality stuffed animal.

Most agree that the best time to play games is during the beginning days of a carnival's engagement. Carnies tend to throw more stock at that time as a method of advertising. Some even go so far as to attach a label to the stuffed animal naming the booth where it was won.

In the waning days of an engagement, in order to boost profits, some operators make their games harder to win. This is especially true if they have had a poor turnout in the early days of the carnival, or if they have awarded more prizes than usual.

People sometimes complain about how seedy carnies are. Indeed, some carnies are itinerant workers who lead a hand-to-mouth existence. Some even sleep in their joints, although this is discouraged by carnival owners. Some have criminal records and find a carnival a perfect way to make some money without having to prove an identity. But many carnies are very much like any other small-business operators one would find in any town in the United States.

Yet the author has seen members of the public act disgracefully toward carnies for no good reason. He saw one rowdy stand in front of a booth and verbally abuse the carny when asked politely to move on. He saw another player threaten a carny after he lost. And he saw a third carnivalgoer cheat at the game when the carny wasn't looking.

Carnies also complain about how many people steal from the booths.

The Golden Rule should reign on the midway: treat a carny as you wish to be treated. But at the same time, don't be intimidated. This book encourages people to ask questions politely about the game before handing over any money. Ask to see the game demonstrated, ask to examine a target and the projectile, ask what size prize one receives for winning the first time.

If the carny becomes surly because you are asking so many questions, simply move on. One Bushel Basket game the author observed had a sign stating "No Stupid Questions." The carny working the game was an "alibi agent," an operator specializing in cheating people who won honestly by saying they went too far over the foul line, the shot was on the rim, etc. When it is your money, there are no stupid questions.

Don't accept an invitation from the carny to cheat. That's called fairbanking, and you'll wind up the loser in the end. Never give the carny more money at one time than the game costs to play.

This book suffers from the inevitable flaw of overgeneralization. There is no regulation-sized Roll Down, or Milk Bottle game, or Fish-Up Bottle. Carnival games, almost by definition, are simple to operate and simple to make.

Consequently, many games are homemade, and operators change the game's dimensions and paraphernalia to suit themselves. Some games are manufactured by reputable companies such as Acme Premium Supply Corp. and Bob's Space Racers Inc. Having a label from a reputable manufacturer helps, but it isn't the final word. Even games that were legitimate to start with can be gaffed, as the carnival industry concedes.

Finally, carnivalgoers should enjoy the sights and sounds of the midway. The intention of this book is to educate the public so it can reward honest carnies by playing their games and drive flatties from the midway. But the book would have the wrong effect if it created a jaded public that stopped playing the games altogether. The carnival is an American tradition that should be passed down to our children.

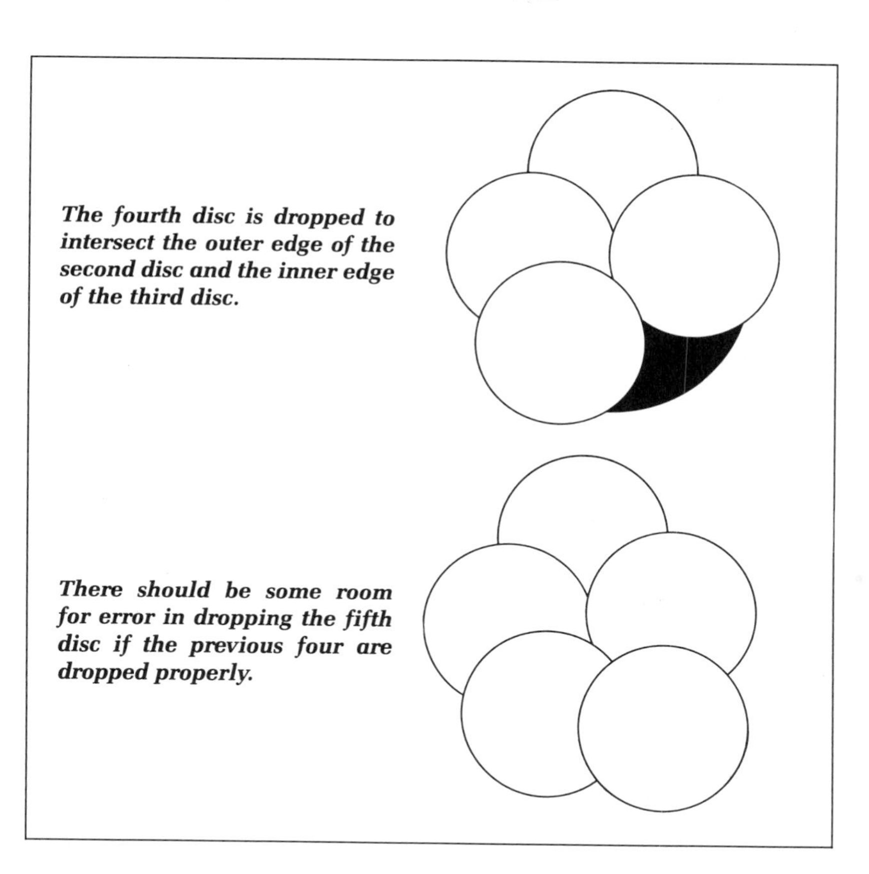
The fourth disc is dropped to intersect the outer edge of the second disc and the inner edge of the third disc.

There should be some room for error in dropping the fifth disc if the previous four are dropped properly.

the board to see if they are all round. If one or more appear elongated, don't play. Note whether the operator uses the heel of his hand to cover part of the spot showing during the demonstration.

Don't accept the challenge from a carnie who drops four discs and offers to let you drop the fifth one at a higher price than the normal game. A Federal Bureau of Investigation bulletin describes a couple of ways an operator can cheat players with this come-on. In one method that employs misdirection, the operator spreads the four discs on the board slightly with his thumb and index finger as he offers the fifth disc to a player with the other hand.

Some operators say a player must drop the disc from a height of six inches or more; others say it is all right for a player to rest the heel of his hand on the board during play and drop the discs from a height of one inch. Obviously, it is easier to win the game if you drop the discs from a lower height.

EAU CLAIRE DISTRICT LIBRARY

Carnies depend on the tendency of the lightweight magnesium-zinc alloy discs to float as they drop, thereby ruining a player's accuracy. That is why drops from one inch are much more accurate than drops made from six inches.

Different operators at the same carnival play the game differently, so look for the one who has more lenient rules. Ask the operator to demonstrate the legal height. That will deter "alibi agents", those who deny prizes won legitimately by telling players they violated the rules.

John Scarne, the gambling expert, found that he was able to drop a disc correctly from a height of six inches about one out of every three tries. He went on to figure that the probability of a player dropping five discs correctly for a win was one in 243 tries.

However, the author has won Cover the Spot at various carnivals much more easily than Scarne calculated. The minimum number of tries it took the author to win was four, and the maximum number was 12. In all those cases, the rules of the game allowed a player to rest the heel of his hand on the board, and drops could be made from a height of one inch.

Before playing, the author practiced for a few hours on a game he made at home from everyday materials.

How to Make Your Own Game

Here are plans for two versions, one fashioned from cardboard, which will suffice for practice; and the other, a deluxe model made of wood and sheet metal that will give the same feel as an actual carnival game.

Materials and tools needed for cardboard game: compass, ruler, scissors, any color felt-tipped marker, one sheet of cardboard 1 foot square, and five sheets of cardboard 5 inches square. Cardboard from a clothing gift box works well.

Draw a 6½-inch-diameter circle in the middle of the 1-foot-square cardboard, and double check its size with the ruler. It is important that the circle be exact.

Color in the circle with the felt-tipped marker, taking care that the color stays inside the compass line. This will serve as the game board.

Draw a 4-inch-diameter circle on each of the five cardboard sheets, again using the ruler to be sure that all the circles are exact. With the scissors, cut around the circles exactly on their circumferences. You now have a complete game for practice.

Materials and tools needed for deluxe game: compass, tin snips, small nail, hammer, ruler, white paint and a contrasting-color paint, model brush and 1-inch paint brush, one sheet any thickness plywood or wood 1 foot square, and one sheet of easily cut sheet metal or zinc 9½ inches square. Sheet metal used for heating ductwork can be obtained at a hardware store and will suit the purpose.

First, paint the plywood white. When it is dry, draw a 6½-inch-diameter circle in the middle of the square. Double check the diameter with the ruler. With the model brush and a different color, paint the circumference of the circle, taking care not to go outside of the line. Then paint the inside of the circle with the wider brush. This will serve as the game board.

With the nail and hammer, make a small dent in the sheet metal about 2¼ inches from the top and side edge of the sheet metal. Since the small dimple is used only to keep the compass point from traveling, it should not be deep or noticeable.

Draw a 4-inch-diameter circle with the compass, and double check the diameter with the ruler. Draw four more circles on the sheet metal following the above procedure; they can be drawn anywhere space allows. Try to keep the circles within ¼-inch of each other.

Wearing leather gloves or some other protection and working carefully with the snips, cut the sheet into squares, with each square containing a circle. Then try your best to follow the pencil line, bending back scrap metal with pliers as it forms. It is better to cut a little more than necessary outside of the circle, and then file or sand the disc to roundness.

Again, work slowly so as not to cut yourself on the sharp metal. Dispose of the scrap metal in a safe manner so others will not accidentally cut themselves.

Wearing leather gloves or other protection, smooth the edges of the discs with fine sandpaper, making sure all the sharp edges are dulled. People will be handling the discs, and you don't want anyone to be cut.

You're ready to play!

Chapter 3

Coin-Operated Carnival Games

There's nothing like a Skill Crane or a Bulldozer to grab the attention of youngsters visiting a carnival midway. Peer inside the window of one of these games, and you'll see a virtual toy store of trinkets children love: miniature guns, stuffed toys, jackknives, novelty banks and toy cars.

The price is right for the parents: usually a quarter per play for Skill Crane or a dollar for seven tokens for Bulldozer. The skill or talent involved in winning is minimal, often consisting of no more than cranking a handle, dropping tokens into a slot or pushing buttons. But the chance of winning varies greatly with the type of game played.

If you are interested in keeping children busy or whiling away some time yourself, by all means play the coin-operated amusements. They are inexpensive entertainment and you may win a prize. But these are not games of skill. Winning rests largely on your luck.

However, there are a number of more sophisticated, electronic cranes entering the midway that are dependent on skill. They cost more to play than old-style amusements such as the Skill Crane, but that is the price one pays for better odds at winning.

Skill Cranes, Drag Lines, Diggers and Steam Shovels

Considered to be one of the granddaddies of coin-operated amusements, the Skill Crane found on some of today's midways made its appearance in the early 1920s.

Electronic cranes are replacing old-fashioned, crank-operated cranes on the midway.

To operate this game, the player inserts a coin in a slot and turns a crank that starts the toy crane moving.

The crank controls how far the crane rotates over the prize field, drops the shovel and retrieves the prize – virtually leaving no skill to the player. A player cannot move the crane in any direction except forward.

Gears that move the crane are programmed to drop the shovel at one of six to eight positions, so it is extremely difficult to win prizes between those stops. Some carnies advise that a player can win prizes between the programmed stops by turning the crank rapidly, causing the shovel to swing and drop after the boom reaches its scheduled stop.

The speed at which the jaws of the shovel close is controlled by the crank, so the player can make the shovel snap shut or close gently over a prize.

But when it comes down to it, the Skill Crane is a game of luck. In its early days, when the prizes were more likely to be gold or silver coins, the game was gaffed by pushing sought-after items deep into carpeting so the shovel couldn't grasp them.

Law enforcement agencies report that the jaws of the crane may be too weak to pick up heavy objects or too small to pick up large prizes. The Kansas Bureau of Investigation has found games that use a slip gear to pull the crane's boom back as the shovel is lowered.

Probably the most scientific examination of the Skill Crane was conducted by the engineering school at the University of Regina in Regina, Saskatchewan, in August 1976 for the Royal Canadian Mounted Police. The mounties had seized a Skill Crane in Swift Current, Saskatchewan, earlier in the year and asked two engineering professors to assess "the probable success rate for a player."

A total of 18 people ranging in age from 9 to 43 played two Skill Cranes a total of 1,352 times, the university's report states. The players succeeded in picking up a prize and dropping it in the retrieval area on only about 11.2 percent of all tries. That means the odds of winning were about 1 in 9, and "the average person would have to invest at least 75 cents to obtain a prize" in a machine that cost a dime for one play, a quarter for three.

Regina Professors P. Bhartia and R. Moffat also noted that success in picking up a prize was largely determined by its shape and its position in the shag carpeting.

Players had the best luck picking up objects with small, irregular shapes, such as a glass vase, horse or barrel. The players had difficulty picking up a pen, can opener, cigarette lighter, coin or knife.

Making certain assumptions – for example, that each machine

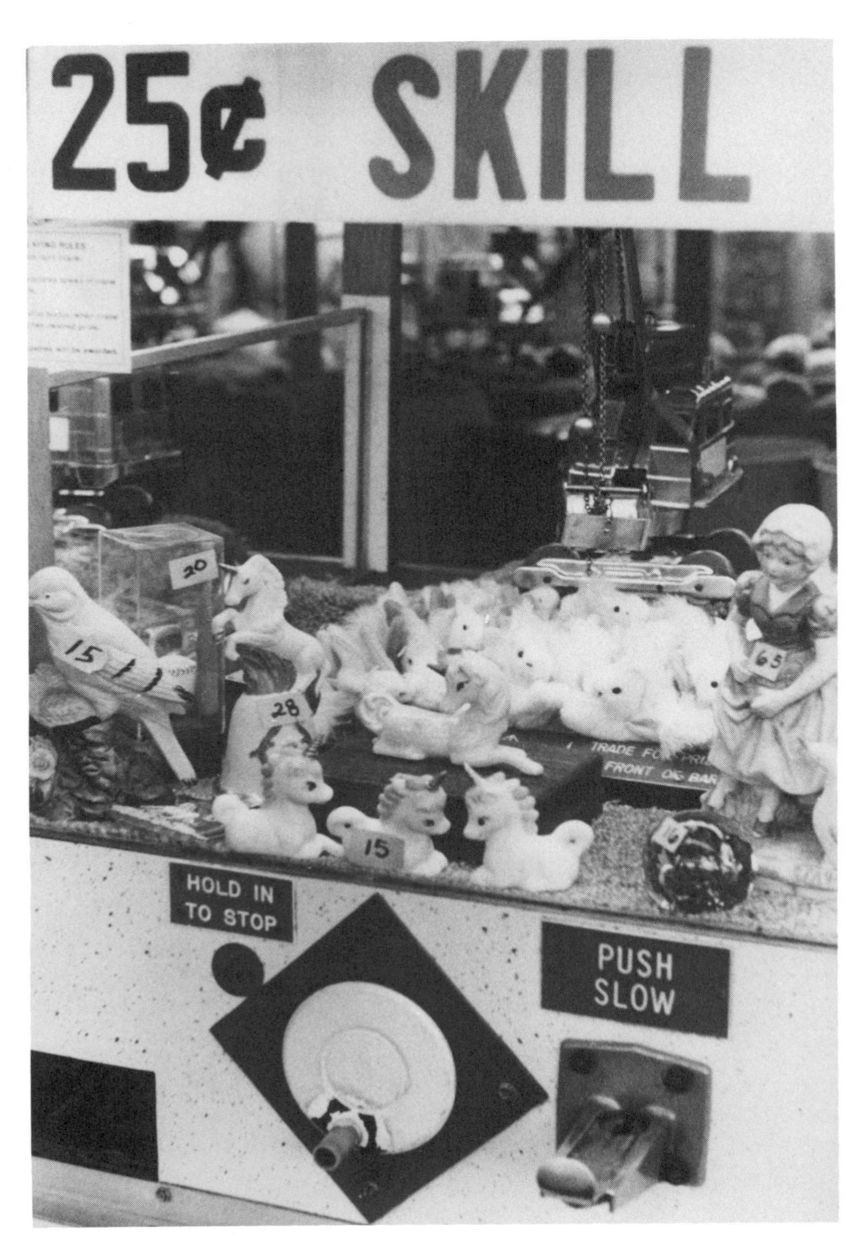

Most crank-operated cranes today have a button that stops and drops the claw, adding an element of skill that earlier crank-operated versions neglected.

would be active only one-quarter of the time – the study suggested that gross income per machine would be approximately $2 per hour. "This appears to be a small sum," the study said, "but if you consider an operator owning 30 machines and operating 10 hours per day for 100 days, this works out to a gross income of $60,000 per year."

Most Skill Cranes found on the midways these days have buttons that control when their buckets are lowered. One carny who used to make Skill Cranes told the author that the buttons add a greater skill element, but game operators take in less money per hour because players use more time trying to get desired prizes. He added, however, that the button modification on the older machines was necessary to permit their use in certain states as games of skill.

Bobby Keelyn, service manager of Universe Affiliated International Inc. in Wall, N.J., cautions that players cannot get prizes in "dead spots" – areas in the display case, usually near the windows, where the crane's claws cannot reach. Operators sometimes lure players with a display of expensive prizes in the dead spots, "but reputable carnival owners will place those same prizes in the areas the claw can reach," Keelyn says.

He says many of the old-style mechanical cranes are still in operation, and have paid for themselves many times over. "A lot of people are looking for these types of cranes," Keelyn says. "Doctors use them in their offices, people have them in their rec rooms. There is a lot of nostalgia associated with the machines."

Newer, electrically driven cranes sold by Universe Affiliated are dependent on skill; consequently, they cost more to play. The claws of the crane are powered by electric motors, and the controls are electronic. Most of the cranes have only a one-way action, Keelyn says, but some games allow players to move the claw back and forth. However, there is a time limit on the two-way cranes.

The operator usually pays out from 20 percent to 30 percent of the gross collections in prizes, Keelyn says. Prizes cost anywhere from 30 cents to $1.50, and the machines can be adjusted to take 50 cents, 75 cents or $1 per play.

"The play of the game depends on hand-eye coordination," Keelyn says. "The average player should be able to capture his prize in one to six tries."

Keelyn offers three pieces of advice for players:

- Try to determine the angle at which the prize is lying before you play. Go after the prizes that aren't lying at angles that make them difficult to pick up.
- Try to get the claws of the crane all the way around the prize, rather than just on the end or tip of the stuffed animal.

• Make sure the prize you want is not in a dead spot.

William Riedthaler, special deputy with the Cuyahoga County Sheriff's Office in Cleveland, contends in a study he conducted in March 1987 that it is largely a matter of luck that players win at some electric cranes. With an electric crane, the player inserts money and presses buttons or swivels a joystick that controls the motion of an electrically powered claw.

In his analysis of one model of the Big Choice crane, Riedthaler found that the machine had a considerable number of dead spots, that prizes were packed too tight to be won, and that the claw's grip was too weak for the machine to pick up large prizes.

Riedthaler says that prizes could be won in only about 33 percent of the machine's playing field because the claw could not reach areas close to the sides of the machine. Larger prizes were placed in the dead spots, giving a player the mistaken impression that he or she could win those prizes, the study said.

To make winning even more difficult, prizes that the claw could reach were packed too tightly to be dislodged, Riedthaler says.

The machine used a Belgium cradle mechanism that has three polished metal fingers to grasp objects. The grip of the electric-powered claw was adjusted on its weakest setting, making it impossible for

This side spill, labeled "out of bounds," drains away a good percentage of tokens used in playing Bulldozer. Some law enforcement agencies require Bulldozer and Penny Fall operators to post signs that draw attention to the existence of side spills.

the claw to pick up larger prizes, the study said. At the same time, the claw's tracking system was so jerky that prizes that had been retrieved sometimes fell out before the claw reached the prize chute.

An official of the company that makes the Big Choice crane, Betson Enterprises, a division of H. Betti Industries Inc. in Moonachie, N.J., was quoted in a magazine article as saying that the machines can be adjusted so they pay out in prizes anywhere from 18 percent to 40 percent of the money taken in by the operator.

A Betson Enterprises spokesman says he was familiar with Riedthaler's study and took no issue with it. He says the machine analyzed by Riedthaler is legal in many states, and that his company has made other models that correct some of Riedthaler's criticisms.

Art Werner, vice president in charge of redemption games for Betson Enterprises, says the company advises operators that, if they want to be successful, they should give people a fair chance to win. A person carrying a prize on the midway is the best advertisement a carny can have, he says.

The company dissuades operators from stuffing prizes in too tightly or turning down the claw's control so it cannot pick up heavier prizes, Werner says.

In early 1985, Betson Enterprises came out with its California model, which allows players more control over the movement of the claw and does not use an electric control to adjust the claw's grip. Werner defended the use of a grip control because the machines are made to take a variety of prizes, some of which could be damaged by a claw exerting too much pressure.

The California model, so called because it satisfies regulations set by that state, also identifies the dead spots in the playing field with stainless-steel partitions.

Betson Enterprises also builds a model that essentially has no dead spots, Werner says. A third model uses a joystick and a mechanism that can be moved precisely where the player wants, but players must accomplish the task within a certain time limit.

Bulldozers and Penny Falls

Like the old-style Skill Cranes, the Bulldozer and the Penny Fall are not primarily games of skill. Penny Falls were invented in England about 1955 and made their way to American midways in the early 1970s. They were dubbed Penny Falls because they originally operated on the English half pence, which is about the same size as the U.S. quarter.

The Penny Fall pushes coins or tokens from left or right, while its American cousin, the Bulldozer, pushes coins toward the player.

To operate a Bulldozer or Penny Fall, the player inserts coins or tokens vertically into a long, narrow chute that pivots. The pivot allows players to aim where they want their coins or tokens to land on the playing field below, once they travel through the chute.

An arm the width of the playing field sweeps back and forth a few inches on one end of the field. On the other end of the field is a ledge. Players can retrieve prizes, coins or tokens after they fall off the ledge.

Theoretically, the player is able to use the chute to drop new coins or tokens on the playing field in such a way that they will push prizes or other coins over the ledge. But the game features three arrangements that can prevent the player from winning: side spills, a beveled or roughened lip on the ledge, and the weight of the prizes.

Side spills are slots on both sides of the field that bleed off coins directly to the operator. Some of the slots are adjustable, so an operator can determine the percentage of take from those playing the game. The side spills are sometimes difficult to see because they are obscured by prizes.

If players look carefully, they can see both side spills on a Bulldozer, because the sweeping action of the game is toward and away from the player. But in a Penny Fall, players may not be aware of the second slot because the action of the game is from left to right.

To make it even more difficult for players, operators sometimes place a beveled lip on the ledge or roughen the ledge. When operators use a lip, coins or tokens must travel up a slight incline to fall. When the lip is beveled or the ledge roughened, coins cannot slide freely over the edge. Since it is harder to push the coins or tokens over the edge in both cases, more tokens fall into the side spills.

Unscrupulous operators will arrange stacks of coins or tokens near the ledge to make it seem they are on the verge of falling into the hands of players. But the weight of the stacks prevents them from being moved by coins or tokens dropped behind them.

A study by Riedthaler of a Penny Fall confiscated by the police department of North Olmstead, Ohio, showed that players may spend up to $16 for a prize necklace valued at $1. The study, conducted in August 1979 on a Sweepstakes game manufactured by the Gold Coast Coin Co., indicated that 40 percent to 50 percent of all the tokens go directly to the operator via the side spills.

Through a series of trials, Riedthaler found that the average player wins back about 19 tokens after dropping 50 tokens down the chute. At that rate, and assuming that all tokens won would be replayed, it would take 608 tokens to win a radio valued at $8.

Most carnies rule that once tokens are purchased for 25 cents, they cannot be redeemed for cash.

The study also found that players could better their averages somewhat by dropping six or seven tokens quickly down the chute before the arm swept back. If a player drops only one token at a time, between 50 percent and 60 percent of the tokens fall in the side spills. If the player drops six or seven tokens at a time before the arm sweeps, only 40 percent to 50 percent of the tokens fall into the side spills. Consequently, look for the newer and fairer games with buttons that stop the sweeping motion while tokens are inserted.

Law enforcement agencies across the country have frowned upon Penny Falls and Bulldozers because the games can be so misleading. To combat the deception, some agencies have required carnival operators to post prominent signs that warn about the side spills or lips.

Signs that appeared at the Michigan State Fair in Detroit read: "Tokens falling into sides – out of bounds – are retained by operator. Use timing and skill to push black tokens (player's choice of prize) and prizes off front edge toward you. Some use red lip that make it harder."

The author wrote a letter to the address posted on a sign that offered to provide more information, but got no a response.

Chuck Schofield, lieutenant with the Peoria County Sheriff's Department in Peoria County, Ill., says his agency requires that operators of Bulldozers at the Heart of Illinois Fair post signs explaining the games, and make the side spills "totally evident" to the players. Operators even use masking tape arrows that point to the side spills, Schofield says.

U.S. District Court Judge Michael Mihm, who was an Illinois state attorney for Peoria County when it started examining carnival games at the fair, says notices have been required since 1973, so that players are more aware of their chances.

Chapter 4

Bottle Set-Up

From a distance, the Bottle Set-Up game appears to be something like a fish pond, where players seek some sort of "catch" using poles with lines attached to the ends. In this case, the catch is an empty beer bottle or soda bottle, and the bait is a wooden or plastic ring attached to the end of the line.

The object of the game, also known as Fish-Up Bottle, is to bring upright a bottle lying on its side by slipping the ring over its neck and raising the end of the stick. The bottle rests on a stand about a foot square and a few inches above the ground. Players are not allowed to shorten the string by wrapping it around the pole. And if the bottle rolls off the stand, the player has lost the game.

Bottle Set-Up is primarily a game of skill. The author has seen one carny – using the same equipment as players and standing in their spots – right eight bottles in a row simply because of his skill. As with any carnival game, Fish-Up Bottle can be gaffed. But for the most part, the games are fair, and your chances of winning increase with practice.

After the author made a game and practiced, he found he could win at some Bottle Set-Ups in only one try. He also acquired enough experience to know after one try which Fish-Up Bottles were too difficult for him to win.

The Secret

In order to right the bottle, the player has to make the neck of the bottle move in an arc – so his or her hand has to move up and back in

Bottle Set-Up is a game of skill that takes good hand-eye coordination and plenty of practice.

an arc. The bottle cannot be made to stand by pulling it straight up or straight back.

The motion of lifting the bottle should be firm and constant, not a jerking movement. Jerking either makes it impossible to control where the bottle is going or gives it so much momentum that it topples.

The bottle should be lifted so that it moves directly toward the player.

Make a fist around the stick at its halfway point and hold it nearly vertical. Keeping it that way, place the entire stick inside the barrier of the carnival stand. Position the pole over the bottle as it lies on the board, and slip the ring over its neck.

Some people prefer the neck of the bottle pointing toward them, and some would rather have it point away from them. It depends on what a person feels comfortable with and whether the board is level. If a board is not level, the bottle neck should be swung uphill.

After slipping the ring over the bottle neck, a player should lift the pole a couple of inches. Take care not to lift so high that the ring slips off the bottle. It is impossible to say how high the pole should be raised because carnies use bottles that differ in length and lip shape; but experience will teach players the correct height.

Bring the pole directly toward you in an upward arc, holding your fist steady. If the tip of the pole moves to your right or left during this motion, the bottle will swerve to one side, rather than come toward you. Once it reaches a certain angle in relation to the board, the bottle will almost right itself.

Words of Caution

The game is played on a foot-square board or octagon that is covered with Formica or another hard, slick substance.

Tom Dawson, chairman of Acme Premium Supply Corp., a St. Louis supplier of carnival games, advises that the playing surface, bottle and rings should be free of wax or grease. The bottle should be placed in the middle of the board, which should be level.

The string should not be more than 54 inches or less than 36 inches, and the pole should not be more than 36 inches or less than 24 inches.

It is much more difficult to win if the board is not level. You can get a fairly good idea about whether the playing surface is level by looking for shims under the board. If the shims appear to make the board tilt markedly, you may want to find another game. There may be other Bottle Set-Up joints at the same carnival that offer smaller prizes but a more even chance for you to win. Again, ask the carny to

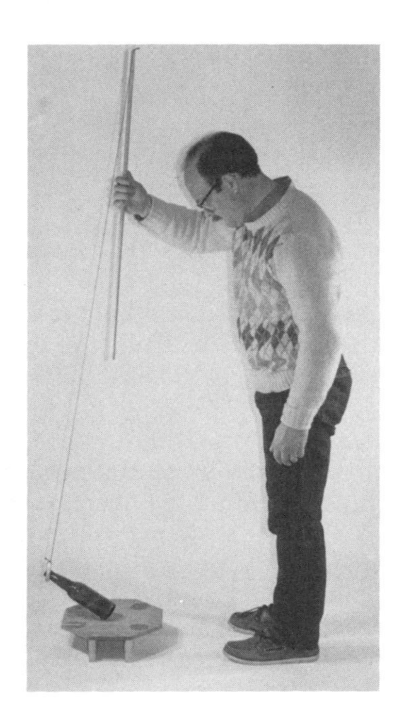

Players should grasp the pole at its middle and hold it close to vertical, as the author demonstrates here. Position the pole directly over the bottle at the beginning of play.

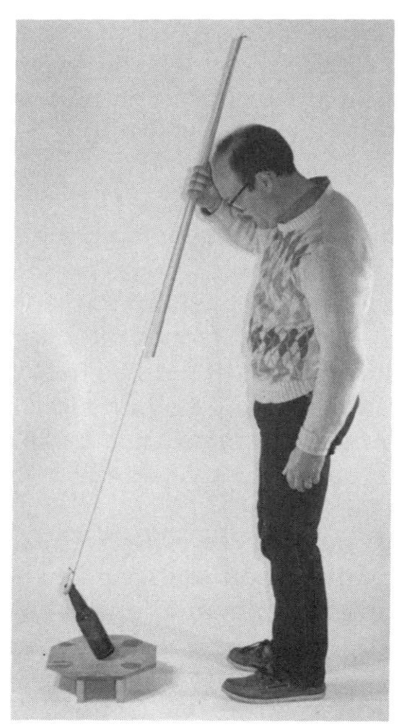

The pole should be brought directly toward the player's body in an arc.

demonstrate before you play.

Law enforcement agent Schofield says some carnies have laid the bottle on its side in such a way that its weight shifts, making the task of righting the bottle even more difficult. He says the heavier side of the bottle tends to be the side with the manufacturing number, so some carnies will turn the number up to distribute the weight unevenly.

However, it seems unlikely that this is a common practice, and a good player can still compensate for the shift in weight.

How to Make Your Own Game

The best way to master the Bottle Set-Up is to make a game at home and practice it until winning becomes second nature. All of the materials needed to make a Bottle Set-Up can be found around the house and at a hardware store. The game takes only a few hours to construct, and it can be an entertaining stunt to show others and fun to play in leisure hours.

Materials and tools needed: saw, hammer, straightedge, tape measure, a few 4d smooth or finish nails, 1-foot-square sheet of any thickness particle board covered with Formica laminate (shelving material works well), two boards ¾-inch thick by 2¾-inches wide by 6 inches long, two boards ¾-inch thick by 2¾-inches wide by 3 inches long, 3-foot-long dowel that is ½-inch diameter, small nail, a piece of fishing line or string 5½ feet long, wooden curtain ring with an inside diameter of about 1⅝ inches, and long-neck beer or soda bottle.

Start with a 1-foot-square sheet as the top of the board; hardware stores sell single sheets of shelving covered with Formica that work well.

It is perfectly fine if you want to keep the board square; some carnies build their games this way. If you want a version that is tougher to win and more representative of the midway, you can make an octagon-shaped board by marking points 3½ inches from each corner on all four edges, drawing lines to connect the eight points, then sawing off the four triangular ears. You can prevent splintering of the Formica when you saw by placing masking tape on both faces of the board and drawing the guidelines on the masking tape.

To make the base for the playing surface, make a rectangular box by nailing together the two 6-inch-long boards and the two 3-inch-long boards.

Drive a small nail into one end of the dowel and attach one end of the string or fishing line. On the other end of the line, about 54 inches from the end of the pole, attach the wooden curtain ring.

Lay a bottle on the board and you are ready to play. To guard against the bottle breaking when it rolls off the playing surface, you may want to place a cloth or other padding beneath and extending beyond the board.

Chapter 5

Shooting Galleries

Although it's one of the most entertaining amusements on the midway, the game in which players attempt to shoot out a paper target using an air-powered machine gun is difficult to win.

The object of the game is for the player to shoot out a red star printed on a counter-level paper target at a range of about eight feet, using No. 2 or No. 1 lead shot.

A cousin to the star game is Shoot Out the Dots, which uses special .22-caliber bullets to tear out a target. Shoot Out the Dots is falling from favor on the midway because the game sometimes is outlawed in cities that have ordinances against discharging firearms in their jurisdiction. At best, Shoot Out the Dots is an extremely difficult game to win.

Star Game

The star game is a tough game to win, according to Bob Snyder, president of a Walnut, Calif., gaming consultant business that bears his name.

Snyder and others say the best technique is to shoot a circle around the paper star, essentially cutting it out with the pellets. It is important to note that all of the red must be shot from the paper to win.

The player's odds of winning depend on the size of the target, the type of paper on which the target is printed, the number of pellets provided, and the air pressure and mechanical condition of the gun.

A study indicates that players successfully shoot out a 1-inch star an average of eight times in 1,000 tries.

As the star gets larger, players have a more difficult time winning. The odds of winning drop slightly for this 1⅛-inch star.

A thin-arm version of a 1⅛-inch star.

For a 1¼-inch star, players win about three times in every 1,000 plays. (Stars courtesy of William Riedthaler)

Something as simple as using a ¼-inch larger target can vastly change the odds of winning.

According to Snyder, the best information on the odds of winning the star game was collected in the late 1970s by Magic Mountain Theme Park in Valencia, Calif., a major amusement park. The park ran several of the games and kept track of how many prizes were awarded in 750,000 plays.

When the game used a five-pointed star measuring 1 inch from point to opposite point, the number of winners averaged eight for every 1,000 plays.

The park once ran low on 1-inch stars and borrowed some 1¼-inch stars from another midway, Snyder says. In the week that it used all the same equipment except for the stars, the park found it paid off only three wins for every 1,000 plays.

Since the odds decreased so much with a 1¼-inch star, Snyder suspected that it would be almost impossible for the average player to shoot out the 1½-inch star some midways were using. Snyder, then a supervising sergeant with the Los Angeles County Sheriff's Department, took one operator who was using the 1½-inch star to court to examine the question. The charge was taking money under false pretenses.

At Snyder's request, the FBI laboratory tested the operator's game in 1982 and concluded that the game could be won with 1-inch and 1¼-inch stars as the targets. But games using 1½-inch stars were "almost outright fraud," says William Holmes, supervisory special agent with the gambling unit of the FBI laboratory.

The guns that the FBI tested were fairly accurate, Holmes says. In a test of 100 plays run by the FBI laboratory, investigators found that the guns shot out a pattern spread of about 2½ inches in diameter at a distance of 7½ feet.

What's more, the lab discovered that the type of target paper used could also reduce the chances of someone winning, Holmes says. Investigators had difficulty knocking all the color out of paper with a high fiber content, while paper laced with perforations would tear out in large sections, instead of only in the specific target area.

In his defense, the operator brought in two carnies who – under test conditions set by Snyder – together achieved two wins in 500 shots at 1½-inch stars.

However, Snyder says the men were given optimum conditions under which to shoot, conditions one would not find in a carnival. For instance, the carnies were allowed to examine their targets after firing a few pellets to see what other area needed to be shot out.

Snyder says the operator was convicted by jury trial on the

charges.

Charlie Wagner, general manager of Feltman Products Inc., the Scotch Plains, N.J., company that makes a star game under the name Shoot Out The Star, says the win odds given by Snyder were "ridiculous," but he declined to give what he termed "technical data" on the win odds of his game.

He says Shoot Out The Star originated in 1941, and that it would not have had 2,500 customers in 1987 if it were no good. Wagner also says that many states permit the game and several large amusement parks use it.

Carnival game manufacturer Terry Hampton believed Snyder's win-loss percentages were too low, but he could not give an estimate of the game's odds. He says he didn't recall ever seeing police close down a Shoot Out The Star game in his years as a carny.

A former carny, Hampton is president and owner of Hampton Co. Inc. in Burlington, Mich.

Hampton says it is true that carnies who want to cut back on the number of prizes they award use larger stars, but at the same time, he felt that Shoot Out The Star is one game on the midway he would advise his four children to play.

A 1987 observation of a Shoot Out The Star game tended to support Snyder's figures. In a game that charged $1 to fire a gun loaded with 100 shots, only one win occurred in 261 attempts to cut out a star – with two sides 1¼ inches long and three sides 1³⁄₁₆ inches long – at a distance of about six feet. This game offered only one prize, a medium-sized stuffed animal that wholesaled for about $7.50.

As an aside, Snyder says it usually costs a carny 10 cents per play in materials alone for the star game. That makes it relatively expensive for the carny to operate, considering the operator must pay for stock, privilege, hookup fees, labor and transportation costs before he clears a profit.

Shoot Out the Dots

The object of the game is to shoot out all the red in three to five dots printed on a paper target with soft graphite bullets that disintegrate almost instantly after they leave the rifle muzzle.

Depending on the particular game, the player may be shooting at a distance of four feet to 12 feet, and the target may be dots, stars, airplanes or butterflies.

However, the game is becoming a rarity on the midway. Manufacturers and suppliers of carnival equipment are not very likely to carry the soft graphite bullets that are shot from the smooth-bore,

.22-caliber rifle used in Shoot Out the Dots, Snyder says.

At best, Shoot Out the Dots is extremely difficult, and at worst, the game is a fraud, Snyder says.

He says a former carny testifed in a trial regarding the game several years ago that she never had one winner in the 365,000 plays she had run over 5½ years at an amusement arcade in Long Beach, Calif. Snyder says the game was located on a Long Beach pier frequented by U.S. naval personnel who had experience shooting guns.

Although it appears to depend on marksmanship, the game is almost impossible to win because of the size and composition of the projectile, the paper target, and the size of the dots.

The bullet, called an arcade load, is discharged from the rifle barrel in little chunks, says James Story, detective with the Oklahoma City Police Department. Propelled by a low-powder charge that ranges from a .22-cap to a .22-short, the graphite chunks barely penetrate the target at a range of 10 to 15 feet, Story says.

Even if the bullet remained intact, it would not be able to take out all the red of the .22-caliber-sized dots because its diameter ranges from .15 caliber to .177 caliber. When the carny wants to show players how the dots can be shot out, he makes an impression on the paper target with the bullet casing – which is .22 caliber.

The chunks of graphite tear the paper target instead of punching out a clean hole. Consequently, there is always some red left on the target, even with a direct hit.

In a Shoot Out the Dots game, all the red in the five spots must be shot out with five rounds of ammunition. (Photo courtesy of William Riedthaler)

Story says the physics department of Oklahoma City University was asked in 1986 to analyze the possibility of winning with rifles taken from an arcade at the Oklahoma State Fair in Oklahoma City.

Typically, the object of the game was to shoot out a dot or star with three rounds. After running the test under laboratory conditions, technicians found it would take a minimum of eight rounds to accomplish the task, Story says.

The composition of the paper also affects the odds of winning. One manufacturer of a short-range target boasts in its literature aimed at carnival operators: "We print all targets on our Special Target Cardboard: You pay less prize money with our targets and all our targets are made to 'Look Easy To Win.' "

Chapter 6

Glass Pitch Plate Pitch

The main attraction of Glass Pitch and Dish or Plate Pitch is that these games usually require only pocket change to play, and the prizes awarded range from large stuffed animals to glassware.

At the same time, the games are simple to understand and play: All you do is toss a dime from a distance so that the coin hits and remains on a plate or in a tumbler.

Glass and Plate Pitches can be operated so that they are extremely difficult to win, or they can offer players a fair chance of walking away with a prize. Players can improve their chances with practice, carnies and carnival experts say.

In Glass Pitch, players stand about four feet from a platform that is covered with drinking glasses, china, ashtrays, lamps and other glassware. The floor of the joint is covered with a tarpaulin so coins can be collected easily. The object of the game is to toss a dime so it lands and stays in a glass or on a dish or ashtray. The player who completes a successful pitch gets to keep the target.

In Dish or Plate Pitch, players pitch dimes onto plates that rest about 2½ feet off the ground on the heads of large stuffed animals. If a dime remains on the plate, the player receives the stuffed animal.

The Secret

Former carnies and carnival experts agree that most Glass and Plate Pitches can be won, and say that players can increase their odds of winning by practice. However, they caution that operators

It takes good hand-eye coordination and a light touch to toss a dime so it remains on a glass plate, but it can be done.

can control the amount of stock they give away by the way they set up the game.

In Glass and Plate Pitch, the best pitches are thrown softly in a low arc. Carnival equipment manufacturer Hampton says that if the coin lands flat against the back edge of the plate in Plate Pitch, it will rebound back into the center. He says another way to improve chances of winning is to toss the coin so it travels in a line to other plates if it skips off the first plate.

Carnival consultant Snyder says another way to pitch is to hold the coin between the thumb and forefinger and toss it lightly. He says he has seen some coin-pitch artists hit as many as three tries out of 10.

But no one says Plate Pitch is an easy game to win. During observation of a Plate Pitch game in summer 1987, the author counted eight wins out of a total of 2,865 tosses.

The plates rested atop 22-inch-tall stuffed animals that Acme Premium Supply Corp. sold wholesale that year for about $7.50 each. The closest target was about four feet from the players.

Players tossed dimes at a total of 27 targets – in this case, 11-inch-diameter Fostoria plates billed by Acme Premium as " 'The' plate for the coin-pitch games."

Carnival equipment supplier Dawson says his corporation alters the glass plates for carnival play by placing them in a furnace for 48 hours. The heat causes the sides of the plates to droop, so the surface of the plate is significantly flatter than surfaces on the same style found in stores.

Acme Premium advises operators to set plates on the outside perimeter of the game at an angle of 2 degrees to 3 degrees from horizontal, sloping toward the middle. Another setup suggested by the company has the outer plates about two inches higher than the inner plates. Plates in the center should be exactly horizontal.

But even with special plates and directions on how to use them, Acme Premium cautions operators that Plate Pitch "can be a big loser, so be sure you at least initially keep track of how many prizes you are giving out, compared to how much money is taken in."

If the operator finds that too much stock is being thrown, "increase the difficulty by moving the plates further away from the players and possibly using less plates," Acme says.

How to Build Your Own Game

It is not difficult to set up a practice Plate Pitch at home where a player can get a feel for how the game is won. However, it is best to remember that a player may win more easily at home because of the plate used. Carnival plates are flatter than those obtained in regular

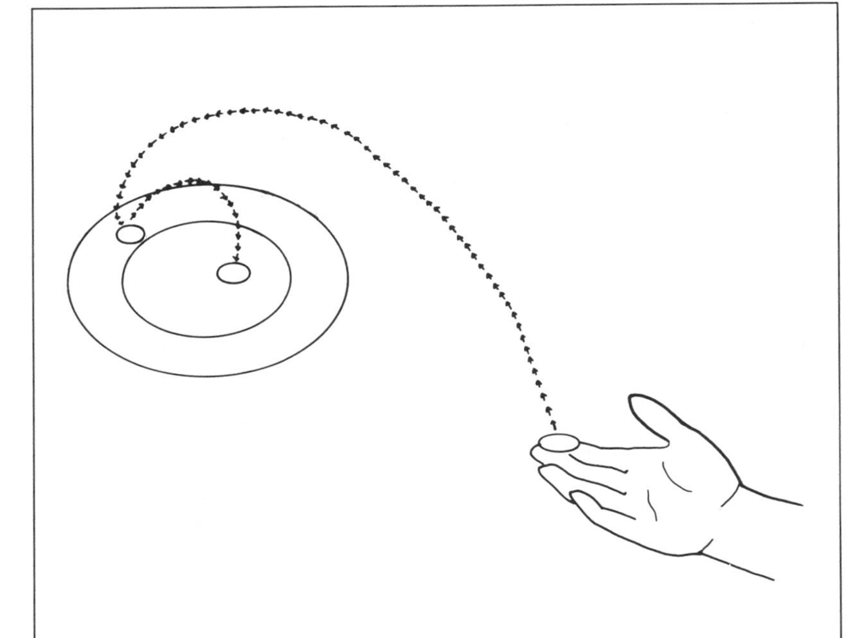

The ideal spot to hit a carnival plate is its far back edge (above). The reason is that a coin that lands perpendicular to the back of the plate will rebound toward the player (below).

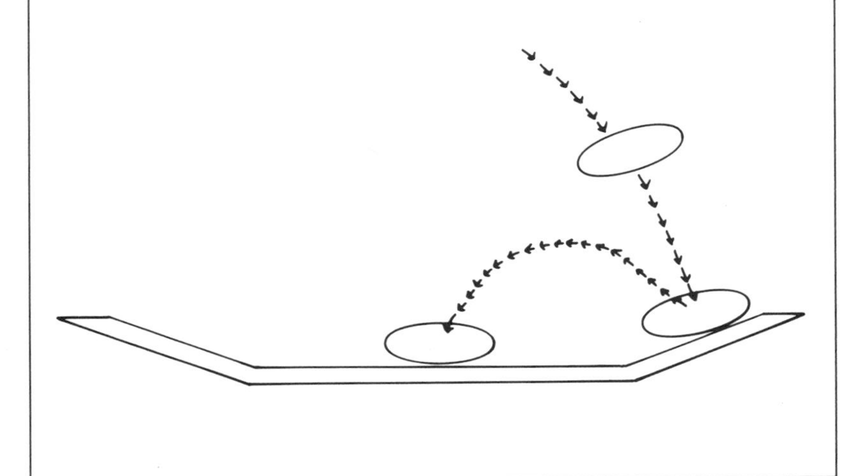

Glass pitches usually are honestly run games in which the player can take home some inexpensive glassware.

stores.

Use a glass plate 9 to 11 inches in diameter that is nearly flat but has sides rising at a slight angle. Some salad plates fit this description well.

Lay a blanket or tarpaulin on the floor to catch coins and set the plate on some object so it stands about 2½ feet high. Toss coins from a distance of at least four feet. If you don't have much change around, buy a couple rolls of dimes from your local bank.

One carny says the following is a good pitching method: Hold the hand out flat, palm up. Balance a dime on the tip of the middle finger. Slowly swing the hand, bending the elbow and using the whole arm. Toss the coin so that it sails without spinning or wobbling and lands flat against the back edge of the plate.

If the pitch is done correctly, the dime will hit the back edge and bounce forward into the middle of the plate. You should be able to get several dimes on the plate after a couple hundred throws.

Words of Caution

Carnies readily admit they can increase the number of prizes they give out by packing the prize animals together, or cut back the number of prizes by spacing the animals out. The spacing determines the chances of coins rebounding off a plate and landing on another plate.

Operators use relatively large plates to give the impression that the game can be won easily, but the important element is not so much the size of the plate as the angle at which a coin lands on the plate.

Law enforcement agencies report that some operators spray furniture wax on the dishes and polish them to enhance their slickness, or set the dishes on an angle so coins always slide off.

Some operators of Plate Pitch also control the arc at which coins can be thrown by suspending stuffed animals on a large chain from the center of the joint.

At the beginning of the engagement, when they want to promote more action on the midway, operators make it easier to win by raising the merchandise so players can throw a higher arc. Near the end of the date, the prizes are lowered so players cannot win as easily.

However, several carnies say hanging the prizes does not make nearly as much difference as the spacing of the animals sitting on the ground.

Operators do not allow players to smear the coin with a sticky substance, dirt or spit, so that friction will stop it on a plate.

Another rule is that players can throw only one coin at a time. To get an idea of why operators make this rule, put together the faces of two coins of the same denomination. Hold the coin sandwich on its edges and parallel to the floor. Drop it from a height of about two feet.

If the coin sandwich lands fairly flat on the floor, one coin will remain very near the point directly above where it was dropped. The other coin absorbs more energy and travels farther from the target. Now try exactly the same experiment, but this time use only one coin. You will see that a single coin is much less likely to remain near the target.

Imagine what would happen if a player threw a handful of coins onto a plate in a Pitch game. Some of the coins would deaden the bounce of others, and the operator might be faced with some big payoffs.

Chapter 7

Ring a Bottle

Next time you visit the carnival, count how many Ring a Bottle games are operating on the midway. Most likely, you will find more of these games than just about any other, and for good reason: Ring a Bottle has "flash" in that it offers premium prizes, such as portable stereo radios or huge stuffed animals, yet it appears relatively easy to win.

For $1, the player is given up to seven plastic or hardwood rings that have an internal diameter ranging from 1 3/32 inches to 1 3/4 inches – approximately the size of a curtain ring. The object of the game is to throw a ring over the neck of a soft-drink bottle from a distance of about five or six feet, or drop a ring on the neck of the bottle from a distance of about three feet.

The Secret

This is primarily a game of chance, with odds against the player reaching 580 or 700 to 1, according to the Federal Bureau of Investigation.

FBI investigator Holmes says his department conducted two trial-and-error studies of the Ring a Bottle game in 1978 and 1983 at the request of another law enforcement agency.

In 1983, laboratory technicians set up a game with 480 two-liter, soft-drink bottles, and threw plastic rings commonly used in carnival games a total of 5,520 times. Based upon the results of throws made from five feet, the bureau figured a player's odds of winning

Ring a Coke joints tend to offer the largest prizes on the midway, but the odds are slim that a player will succeed.

the game at about 700 to 1.

In 1978, the laboratory ran a test in which technicians tossed rings with an inside diameter of 1¾ inches from a distance of about six feet onto a square made up of 100 64-fluid-ounce bottles. Each bottle had around its neck a collar about 2 inches in diameter. Out of 7,000 throws, the technicians recorded 12 wins, for a probability of making one shot in every 583 throws.

Holmes says the odds of a player winning get somewhat better if there is no collar and the ring is able to fall entirely down the neck of the bottle. However, charities or church organizations tend to run games with bottles that don't have collars, while professional carnival operators favor bottles with collars.

On closer scrutiny of the results, Holmes' lab found that all of the winning tosses were ricochets. The light, plastic rings would not stay on a bottle even if they were dropped from a height of three inches directly over the neck of the bottle.

"The result is that the game could not be considered a game of skill," Holmes says.

Sgt. Dwain Dennis, detective with the Ionia County Sheriff's Department in Ionia, Mich., says his agency conducted a test of Ring a Bottle on the midway of the Ionia County Free Fair, and came up with similar results.

Dennis says he filled a 10-quart bucket with the plastic rings and threw them all at once on top of the bottles from a regular shooting distance. Only one ring stayed on the neck of a bottle, he says.

It appears that the only way to win the game is to throw a sandwich of two rings at the same time over a bottle neck, Dennis says. However, carnival operators generally forbid throwing more than one ring at a time.

Chapter 8

Skee-Ball

Across the board and without exception, everyone says that Skee-Ball is a legitimate game of skill that employs hand-eye coordination. Since 1909, when the game was invented by J.D. Estes in Philadelphia, it has grown to include a variety of sizes from an amusement park game with 36-foot-long alleys to a 6-foot-long version that can fit in a family's rec room.

The coin-operated version most commonly found on the midway runs from 10 feet to 13 feet in length, and is about 30 inches wide. The object of the game is to roll a baseball-sized wooden or composite ball up an alley and into one of five holes at the end of the ramp. Wooden rings surround each hole. The most difficult hole to hit scores 50 points; the least difficult, 10 points.

Players accumulate points for the prizes they desire, sometimes chalking up enough for such big-ticket items as lamps and toasters.

The Secret

Joe Sladek, president of Skee-Ball Inc. in Lansdale, Pa., says Skee-Ball is a game that employs hand-eye coordination – with a measure of talent thrown in. "Some people who are phenomenal can win after five plays," Sladek says. "Some people like me can play forever and never become good at it."

His company conducted a survey in the late 1950s that indicated the player who rolled nine balls on a 14-foot-long table would get an average score of 240 points. Fourteen-foot-long portable tables are

Skee-Ball has a good reputation as a game of skill, and players usually can trade small prizes for larger ones.

often used at carnivals and amusement parks.

Sladek says the company got approximately the same response when it mailed questionnaires in the late 1970s to amusement parks with Skee-Ball arcades.

He says some players swear that the best technique for hitting the 50-point hole is to throw the ball hard enough so it will fall from the safety net that covers the end of the alley.

Carnival agents are fairly scientific about the way they give out merchandise for Skee-Ball. Skee-Ball Inc.'s literature suggests the 150-30 method of giving out prizes. In this method, the player gets his first ticket that can be counted for prizes when he reaches a score of 150. After that, he receives a ticket for every score over 30.

So the average person playing a nine-ball game would receive four tickets. If the agent wants to return 20 percent of the gross dollars in prizes and he charges $1 per game, each ticket is worth a nickel. He can set the number of tickets needed for various prizes accordingly.

Chapter 9

Group Games

Carnival experts generally agree that group games are perhaps the most honestly run games on the midway and provide the best chance to win large prizes. In a group game, all players pay the same amount of money, and they compete against each other – not the operator. The size of the prize is determined by the number of people playing in a particular round.

For instance, if there are 14 stools at a Kentucky Derby game and all are occupied by players, the operator will offer a large prize to the winner. However, if only seven people are playing, the operator will offer only a small- or medium-sized prize. The operator makes roughly the same percentage of profit regardless of how many people play, and that is why group games tend not to be gaffed.

Carnival expert Riedthaler found that in one Water Balloon Race game where each person paid 25 cents to play, the operator gave out a prize worth about 10 cents wholesale when there were four to six players. When seven to 10 people played, the operator gave out a prize worth about 50 cents. When 11 to 15 people played, a prize valued from $1 to $1.25 was awarded. The large prize, which wholesaled for about $2.25, was given out when 16 to 20 people played.

Since most group games allow a player to trade smaller prizes for larger prizes, group games give the average person a good chance to acquire a large prize.

There is a wide variety of group games, ranging from games that rely strictly on chance, such as Crazy Ball or Wheels, to games that

In group games, such as this Kentucky Derby, players essentially are competing against each other, not the operator.

are largely dependent on skill, such as Kentucky Derby or Water Race. This chapter will devote itself to games that rely on skill.

Derby Race, Kentucky Derby or Horse Race Game

The Derby Race or Kentucky Derby has been on the midway since the turn of the century, but it still captures the attention of carnivalgoers today with the sounds and sights of a miniature horse race.

As you might expect, the object of the game is to make your horse be first over the finish line by rolling a ball into holes in an inclined board or by shooting a ball in a pinball-type arcade. In the turn of the century games, no skill was involved, as the players picked their horses before the game was run.

The Horse Race Game acquired an unsavory reputation over the years because agents could gaff it with relative ease by fixing which horse crossed the finish line first. Some states banished the game from the midway because of this problem.

But the electronic Kentucky Derby is run in a different fashion than the older pinball-type games – so much so that they are similar in name only. A contemporary Derby Race represents a major investment by an operator, and few would jeopardize their livelihoods by rigging a game for a few dollars in prizes.

In other words, an electronic Kentucky Derby is a good bet for the carnivalgoer who seeks a game of skill. Because a prize is given for each race, the probability of winning generally is one (representing yourself) divided by the total number of players, which includes yourself. Those odds can change, depending on the skill levels of the players involved.

The Secret

The secret of winning Kentucky Derby is proper hand-eye coordination, says Terry Hampton, who has been manufacturing the game since 1979. Hampton says it is the most popular of the group games that he manufactures.

Hampton says the object of the game, played on an inclined board, is to roll a golf ball into the hole that carries the most points. Players sit on 14 stools in front of their own boards, each of which has 14 holes. The golf balls roll back to players through a return slot after each shot. Players are not allowed to move their hands beyond a foul line about 1½ feet up from the edge of their boards.

Two red holes at the top of the board are worth the most points; a player who successfully rolls a ball into either of these holes makes his horse move three lengths. The next level has five blue holes, and a ball in any of these makes the horse move two lengths. The six

Water Balloon Race, a favorite on midways for decades, awards various sizes of prizes depending on the number of people playing in a particular round.

yellow holes that line the bottom of the board are worth one length apiece.

"It's a 25-second race, and it's all based on accuracy and quickness," Hampton says. Rolling a ball into a hole approximately twice the circumference of a golf ball takes the same kind of athletic skill that a person hones in playing baseball, basketball and pool.

Most of the games offer winners the option to trade up to larger prizes, and some offer five levels of prizes.

Hampton and Jody Tilton, a carny who owns and operates a Kentucky Derby with a Midwestern carnival, say the average operator gives out from 25 percent to one-third of his gross receipts in merchandise to winning players.

Words of Caution

Law enforcement officials say another type of Horse Race Game that relies on the pinball-type arcade has earned a reputation over the years for being gaffed. Gaming consultant Snyder says pinball-type games are not as common as they were a decade ago, and many of those still operating today no longer have the "G-box," a device that allows the operator to determine by remote control who wins the game.

Snyder says a dishonest operator typically would allow players to win at certain times so they would play longer. For instance, the operator would allow one member of a family to win so that the others would keep playing.

Some law enforcement agencies say a dishonest operator would have a stick, or confederate, sit in with the rest of the players. The operator would then set the machine so the stick would win and return the prize later. Sometimes, an operator of another carnival game would sit in as the stick, and the operator of the Horse Race Game would later visit his colleague's game as a stick.

Water Race

Several carnival experts say they have never seen a gaffed water-race game. In a Water Race, players aim pistols that issue streams of water at the mouths of clown heads revolving slowly from side to side. If a player is an accurate shot, the stream of water will enter the clown's mouth and put pressure on a micro switch. The player who is able to keep the switch depressed longest wins the race.

In Water Balloon Race, the game is over when a player succeeds in bursting a balloon atop the clown's head. Other race games feature frogs, horses, cars or other objects moving along a track.

Bob's Space Racers Inc., a Daytona Beach, Fla., company that bills itself as "America's lead manufacturer of amusement games," makes a water-race game in which cars move along a track. General Manager John Mendes Jr. says winning his company's water-race game depends on a steady hand and a sharp eye to direct the stream of water.

Bob's Space Racers, which specializes in group games for both the carnival circuit and amusement parks, has seen a major change in the carnival industry since the company was established in 1970, Mendes says. "The whole industry has become a fancy way of retailing," he says. "The public demands to be entertained more than it used to."

Consequently, the games have become more sophisticated in their use of lights, sound effects and displays. And costs of the games have risen accordingly. In 1986, the company quoted a price of $51,000 for a 19-seat water-race game contained in a trailer.

Bob's Space Racers manufactures about 20 games, such as Whac-A-Mole, Can Alley, Super Shifter, and Roll-A-Ball horse derby, similar to the one sold by Hampton Co. Mendes says operators of group games give out, on the average, 25 percent to 30 percent of their gross in prizes.

Chapter 10

Roll Down

Roll Down can be found in operation anywhere from a Sunday church bazaar to a state fair. The game has universal appeal for agents because it is easy to set up and run, and there isn't much chance that the players will "beef," or complain, about the outcome.

At the same time, Roll Down is a fun game for players because it is not difficult to learn or to play, and it provides a chance for an average person to win modest prizes. The Roll Downs observed by the author awarded more prizes – albeit small ones – than most other games on the midway. Some Roll Downs are operated as hanky panks, games in which virtually every player wins a prize.

As you might expect, however, it is very difficult for a player to obtain the choice prizes. And carnival experts caution that some games are gaffed so players cannot win the choice prizes.

The object of Roll Down is to get a very high number of points or a very low number of points by rolling balls one at a time into slots at the end of an inclined board. A typical game gives the players six balls, and there are seven or eight slots bearing numbers 1 through 6 over the top of the slots. Games with seven numbers generally have two 3s, and games with eight numbers usually have two 3s and two 4s.

The game ends when all six balls are in slots. The total number of points determines whether the player receives a prize and what size prize is to be awarded.

Though Roll Down may be a common game, it has no standard

The odds of winning a large prize in one play of Roll Down are slim, but players usually can work up to large prizes by trading in smaller ones.

equipment or rules. Some games use five balls instead of six, but there most often are more slots than balls.

A more sophisticated coin-operated game had a playing board 72 inches long and 20 inches wide, and used soft foam-rubber balls that were 8 inches in circumference.

Most operators of Roll Down rely more on games with a volume of customers paying a smaller amount, perhaps 50 cents per play, than games that cater to a few players who spend several dollars apiece at $1 or $2 per play. Roll Down operators keep people playing by offering the incentive of "trade up" – when a player hands over two small prizes for a medium-sized prize, two medium-sized prizes for a large prize, etc.

The Secret

The object of Roll Down is to score either a very high or a very low number of points, and the odds are against you in accomplishing this. To get a feel for how difficult the game will be to win, the player should note the number of balls, the number of slots at the end of the board, and the numbers above the slots.

For instance, the author observed a county fair game that had six balls, eight slots, and numbers above the slots that ran thus: 4, 3, 5, 1, 6, 2, 4, 3. The operator awarded the largest prize for rolling a 6 or 36, and the smallest prize for rolling a 13 or 29.

The operator of that Roll Down game strongly stacked the odds in his favor, because there were two 3 and two 4 slots. Those numbers tend to produce losing scores.

Most Roll Down games use six balls and seven slots bearing numbers 1 through 6 and two 3s. Even with only seven slots in use, the odds of winning are stacked against the player. John M. Dwyer, associate professor of mathematics at the University of Detroit, calculated that there are 117,649 possible combinations in a game with seven slots and two 3s. A glance at the accompanying table of combinations compiled by Dwyer indicates why it is so difficult to win the choice prizes.

In one game the author observed, six balls and seven slots were used, and the player was awarded a small prize worth about 25 cents wholesale if he or she rolled 13 or 14 or 28 or 29. So if skill is not taken into consideration, the probability of a player rolling the above four numbers is about once in every 15 games.

To win a medium prize worth about 50 cents wholesale, the player had to roll 11 or 12 or 30 or 31. If skill is excluded, the probability of a player making any of those four numbers is about once in every 50 games.

ROLL DOWN
Expected Occurrence

Total score	Probability	Prize
6	once in 117,647 plays	Gigantic, worth two Jumbo
7	once in 20,000 plays	Jumbo, worth two Large
8	once in 4,348 plays	Jumbo, worth two Large
9	once in 1,370 plays	Large, worth two Medium
10	once in 510 plays	Large, worth two Medium
11	once in 225 plays	Medium, worth two Small
12	once in 112 plays	Medium, worth two Small
13	once in 62 plays	Small, worth 25 cents
14	once in 38 plays	Small, worth 25 cents
15	once in 26 plays	No prize
16	once in 19 plays	No prize
17	once in 14 plays	No prize
18	once in 12 plays	No prize
19	once in 11 plays	No prize
20	once in 10 plays	No prize
21	once in 10 plays	No prize
22	once in 11 plays	No prize
23	once in 12 plays	No prize
24	once in 15 plays	No prize
25	once in 19 plays	No prize
26	once in 25 plays	No prize
27	once in 37 plays	No prize
28	once in 57 plays	Small, worth 25 cents
29	once in 95 plays	Small, worth 25 cents
30	once in 172 plays	Medium, worth two Small
31	once in 345 plays	Medium, worth two Small
32	once in 752 plays	Large, worth two Medium
33	once in 1,887 plays	Large, worth two Medium
34	once in 5,556 plays	Jumbo, worth two Large
35	once in 20,000 plays	Jumbo, worth two Large
36	once in 117,647 plays	Gigantic, worth two Jumbo

Six balls are rolled onto a table with seven slots bearing numbers from 1 through 6. There are two 3s on the table. Skill is not taken into account.

To win a large prize worth about 75 cents wholesale, the player had to roll 9 or 10 or 32 or 33. Assuming no skill is involved, the probability of the player achieving any of those scores is about once in every 200 games.

To win a jumbo prize worth perhaps $3 wholesale, players must roll 7 or 8 or 34 or 35. The probability of that occurring is about once in every 2,000 games.

To win the gigantic prize worth $5 or more wholesale, the player must roll 6 or 36. If skill is not a consideration, the probability of rolling either of those numbers is one in every 58,825 games.

The author saw players win 11 small prizes in 107 trials – about one winner of a small prize out of every 10 trials – in the above game, which cost 50 cents a play.

It is important here to warn the reader that these calculations of probabilities do not apply to every player and every game. The probabilities given above do not take into consideration the skill of the players, the location of the numbers, the condition of the playing board, etc. The odds may be considerably different for a player who is skilled at Roll Down.

All the consistently good Roll Down players seemed to have a steady hand and a sharp eye. Some place the heel of one hand firmly on the board as close to the foul line as possible, then find the spot where, if they simply release the ball, it will roll to a 1 or 6 slot. They use their free hand to bring the balls to the fixed hand.

Theron Fox, in his book on carnival games, writes that the payoff to players will vary because Roll Down is a game of skill. But he says experience showed that in a game using six balls, seven slots numbered from 1 through 6 with two 3s, and prizes for under 11 or over 30, there will be roughly one winner in every 48 tries. Only one type of prize was awarded in the game.

The game Fox described uses a board about 7 feet long and 2 feet wide. The slots were arranged from left to right in the following order: 3, 6, 1, 3, 5, 2, 4.

Words of Caution

Carnival investigator Riedthaler says it is nearly impossible to hit the highest or lowest numbers in some Roll Downs because the sixth ball will bounce out when it collides with the five already in the slot. He also reported that some boards are warped so certain numbers are favored, and that some balls do not roll true due to ridges around their circumference.

A.B. Enterprizes, in its plans for carnies on how to build a Roll Down, advises that the game can be "made a little more positive to the operator" by constructing the 5, 6, 1 and 2 slots "just a tiny bit narrower" so the difference between them and the normal-sized slots cannot be detected by a player standing six feet away.

A.B. Enterprizes, a Peoria, Ill. company, is known throughout the carnival world for Brill's Bible, a catalog of plans describing the construction of carnival games, rides, magical illusions and midway shows. The descriptions and plans were authored by Aaron K. Brill, founder of A.B. Enterprizes.

Acme Premium Supply Corp., a carnival equipment house, encourages operators to run games where the board is unwarped and all slots are even. It also suggests that the slope of the board be no greater than one inch per foot of board length.

This chapter hasn't concerned itself with another version of Roll Down that was common on midways in the first half of this century. That game used an inclined Roll Down table that had perhaps 36 holes arranged in a square at the bottom of the board, rather than slots.

Each hole carried a number from 1 through 6, and prizes were awarded on the basis of the highest or lowest scores obtained, similar to the way the present-day version of Roll Down is played. However, players usually did not release balls one by one. Instead, all six balls were held on a hinged board at the upper end of the playing board. The player merely lifted up the the board to roll the balls.

Unscrupulous carnies would miscount the balls or push them into holes with middle numbers so the players would get losing scores.

This type of Roll Down may be used today in Razzle Dazzle, a fraudulent carnival game described elsewhere in this book.

Chapter 11

Dart Throws

As is the case with so many other games described in this book, the chances of winning at dart throws depend on the honesty of the operators. Before playing these games, carnivalgoers should exercise some judgment on how tough the game is to win, and whether it is gaffed.

One carny, known among his peers as a successful and honest operator of Bust the Balloon games, put it this way: "There are over a million ways to cheat, but only one way to be honest."

This Indiana carny, who preferred to remain anonymous and has left the business, says players sometimes can discern whether a game is on the up-and-up or dishonest by looking at the prizes.

Legitimate games usually offer reasonable prizes that are little more than carnival souvenirs, such as posters, silk-screened mirrors, T-shirts, stuffed animals and inexpensive toys.

Gaffed dart games generally offer money, television sets and prizes that carry high price tags.

Many of the dart games one finds at a carnival are fair, and players who are skilled at tossing darts have a good chance of walking away with a decent prize.

However, there are two games that players should avoid at all costs: Razzle Dazzle and build-up games.

Under no circumstances should a carnivalgoer play a game in which darts are thrown at a board bearing only numbers, and the numbers selected are then added and converted by use of a chart into

Bust the Balloon can be a good bet for a carnivalgoer who has some skill in throwing darts.

yards of a football game, miles in a road-race game, etc. This is a form of Razzle Dazzle, described in another chapter of this book. It suffices to say that many individuals have been fleeced out of thousands of dollars each in Razzle, the most vicious game to be found on the midway.

In a build-up game, carnies appeal to the gambling nature of the players. Agents encourage customers to keep playing by letting them trade small prizes for larger ones. This sounds much like trade-up, a legitimate way in which players can achieve larger prizes, but there is a crucial distinction. In a build-up game, the prize for a first win is slum, usually hidden under the counter, so a player mistakenly believes that he or she will get one of the choice prizes displayed prominently. It is only after they win that players see the smallest prize.

In games that offer trade-up, the smallest prize and all subsequent prizes are always out in the open, and a sign gives the formula required for all prizes.

Build-up artists also employ a number of ruses to gain the player's confidence. In a con called fairbanking, carnies offer to give players help in the form of free throws or extra points, or even by making a shot for them. This is a classic example of the old adage, "You can't cheat an honest man."

Decline any offers the carny makes to bend the rules of the game.

Carnies also gain the confidence of players by allowing them to win a small portion of their money back so they want to continue playing. In short, never play for money.

Players should examine the darts and gauge whether they will stick in the target or the board itself. Carnival investigator Riedthaler reports that some operators use lightweight darts with needle-like points that cannot penetrate thick plastic targets such as stars.

Finally, pay for each game as you play. Customers who play on credit at the encouragement of the carny often find – to their dismay – that they have spent a large sum of money for an insignificant prize.

Poster Joints, Star Joints, Apple Joints

These games usually are operated honestly, and they demand skill at tossing darts accurately.

Generally, all of the games use regulation darts 5 to 6 inches long, and players stand about six to 10 feet from the targets. The games get their names from the type of target they employ.

In a Poster Joint, players attempt to win a specific poster by hitting the same poster hung on a board. Most players succeed in winning the poster they desire. Poster Joint, which caters largely to children

Star Joints can be games of skill, but players should check whether the darts are heavy and sharp enough to penetrate the targets.

and young adults, is largely a form of retailing. The posters cost the operator perhaps 35 cents wholesale, and the game costs $1 per play. Carnies say the real secret to a profitable Poster Joint is smart merchandising: finding a poster that kids will want, and buying that poster in the largest quantities possible.

Apple Joints employ as a target a red apple with a green stem and leaves. Slum is awarded for hitting the red apple, and a larger prize is given out for hitting the green leaves. Acme Premium Supply, a St. Louis carnival supply house, sells an apple decal about 5 inches in diameter that is almost entirely taken up by the red apple – a relatively good-sized target for a throw of six feet.

Acme Premium suggests to operators that boards be 75 percent covered at all times with apples. The board also should be made of Celotex or other material soft enough to be easily penetrated by darts thrown in a half-circle arc.

The company sells a variety of stars for use in a Star Joint, a game that generally offers better-quality prizes because it relies heavily on the dart-throwing skill of the player. The stars, usually five pointed, range in size from 4 inches to 5 inches, measured from tip to opposite tip.

The stars used in Star Joint often have fairly thin arms, so it is a matter of luck if a carnivalgoer without much athletic skill wins these games. The stars present a good challenge to those who are acquainted with darts.

The player usually throws from a distance of four to six feet, and the game costs $1 per play or $2 for three darts. In one Star Joint observed at a county fair, players made their tosses from a distance of about five feet at stars that measured 5 inches from tip to tip. The plaques awarded for hitting one star cost about 35 cents each wholesale.

Carnies control the game's payout with the type of stars they use and the density of the stars on the board.

Bust the Balloon, Tag Balloon Dart

As the name implies, the object of Bust the Balloon is to toss a dart from a distance of about six to 10 feet and pop a No. 4-, 5- or 7-sized balloon attached by its neck to a board. In a typical 16-foot-long joint, there may be 70 balloons attached to a board, and balloons are about a foot apart from center to center.

Some Bust The Balloon games are run as hanky panks for children; that is, the operator essentially is charging more to play the game than the prizes cost wholesale. Some games guarantee that children under 12 will win a prize.

A successful operator of this type of game has to be a shrewd marketer. The operator has to "buy smart," meaning he or she must buy attractive merchandise at the lowest price possible. Some carnies spend their winters making frames for posters or silk-screening T-shirts to cut down on the cost of attractive prizes.

Bust the Balloon games for adults are run so that prizes are given out according to the number of balloons successfully broken in consecutive hits. In cases where three darts are given for $1, the player usually wins a piece of slum for one balloon, a small prize for two and a slightly larger prize for three.

To win the plush animal displayed in the joint, a player may have to accumulate points by popping several balloons.

As you might expect, players who are skillful at throwing darts have the best chance of winning these games. The best shots have to be thrown fairly hard because balloons for the largest prizes usually are not fully inflated, so they may survive a direct hit with a dart that is thrown lightly. A rule of thumb is that a balloon will be hard to break if it is not translucent.

Balloons that hang from short strings connected to the board are harder to pop because the balloons swing if struck by a glancing blow of the dart.

To get a feeling of the skill required to hit a 5-inch star, copy this reduced photo and attempt to hit it with a dart thrown from a distance of five feet.

Be sure to ask the carny exactly what prize a player receives for the number of balloons he or she breaks. In cases where points must be accumulated for a plush prize, a person may have to break so many balloons that playing the game isn't worth the prize.

Also, examine the darts used in the game. Theron Fox, in his book on how to make money on carnival games, advises operators to twist or trim one of the dart's fins so the dart will "twist in flight and make it more difficult to throw accurately."

Get the rules of the game down before you hand over your dollar. When the carny says "you must break three in a row," ask him whether that means just three balloons consecutively – or whether they also have to be in the same row on the board.

Acme Premium suggests to operators that the target board be 75 percent filled with balloons at all times. The company also stresses that darts must be evenly weighted, with all fins attached and straight.

Tag Balloon Dart is really a game of chance, not a game of skill. Players throw darts at balloons that conceal tags bearing letters or numbers. They are games of chance because players do not know which letter or number rests behind the balloon they are aiming to hit. Although these games can be operated honestly, there is more of an opportunity to rig the outcome than in a Star Joint or other dart games, because the numbers and letters are hidden from the public.

In the S-M-L Dart game, every tag has a letter signifying whether the player has won a small, medium or large prize. Riedthaler says some S-M-L Dart games are very tough, if not impossible, to win. In one game he examined in Cleveland in 1979, there were tags for only six medium prizes and one large prize in the playing field of 72 balloons.

He also says that the medium and large tags were all situated in two columns on the far right and far left ends of the playing field, and agents stood in front of those columns when the game was being played. This made it virtually impossible for a player to win a medium or large prize.

It cost 50 cents per play, and the small prizes were valued at about 6 cents, the medium prizes cost from 10 to 15 cents, and the large prize was worth about $1.25, Riedthaler says.

In A-B-C Darts, players get a small prize if they pop a balloon that has an A tag behind it. To win a medium prize, the player must burst two balloons with A and B tags behind them. A large prize is awarded when three balloons having the A, B and C tags behind them are broken.

Riedthaler says he found in some cases that B or C tags were not on the board at all, or they were situated on the ends of the playing field, as in S-M-L Darts. In some other cases, the tags for medium and large prizes were behind balloons that had already been broken.

Carnival consultant Snyder says some carnies may even palm a winning tag and switch it with a losing tag while they pull the tag from the board. The tags are easily palmed as they are usually about 1 inch in diameter. Snyder says players may even take the word of the carny that they have lost, rather than look at the tag and see for themselves.

In 1-10 Darts, players receive a small prize for any one number, a medium prize for two numbers in a row, and the choice prize for three consecutive numbers. This game is subject to the same gaffs as those described previously. Numbers 3, 6 and 9, or 1, 4, 7 and 10 may be missing from the board altogether, Riedthaler says.

Acme Premium suggests that operators place no major prize winning numbers or colors on the extreme outside rows. It also encourages carnies to have at least four major winning numbers or colors per hundred.

Chapter 12

Cork Gun Galleries

Cork gun galleries remain popular with the public because they have an amusement value over and above the possibility of winning prizes. It's downright fun to sight in on a target and try to blast it off a shelf, even if the prize awarded may be nothing more than slum, such as a pocket comb.

So players shouldn't expect to win large or valuable prizes at cork gun galleries. Some galleries geared for children are inexpensive to play, operate on a shoot-till-you-win basis, and award slum prizes.

Games for adults usually are more expensive to play and offer a set number of shots. Those adult games that offer prizes of value – a cigarette pack with a five-dollar bill wrapped around it, or an all-metal lighter – most likely are too difficult to win, carnival experts say.

There are some rules of thumb a player can use to judge whether a game can be won and optimize his or her chances of winning. Take a few moments to observe the layout of the game. Check to see where the targets are situated on the shelves and whether they are weighted. Go so far as to ask to handle a target or two before handing over your dollar.

Be wary of games where a prize of value is attached to the target that must be knocked over. Often, the prizes make the targets so heavy that the game cannot be won.

One general rule is to select the newest-looking gun, if there is a choice. Older airguns generally have worn pistons and lower com-

This target joint was run as a shoot-till-you-win game, but it was unlikely that players could win much more than a comb because of the way the targets were constructed.

pression. Consequently, they don't put enough power behind the cork to enable it to keep a true trajectory and knock over targets.

Also, examine the sights on the gun and the corks used. A.K. Brill, in his plans for carnies on how to build cork gun galleries, suggests that "the first thing a good operator must do to make a profit is to reset the sights so they are not accurate and spot weld the change in place."

Operators tend to use a gun such as a Daisy Model 25 rifle, a quality airgun made by Daisy Manufacturing Co. Inc. in Rogers, Ark., that shoots No. 3 corks. Brill advises that the Daisy guns are straight shooters, but "in order to make the targets hard to hit, you twist the sights."

"You can offer good prizes because with jammed sights, they (players) are not going to hit very often," he writes.

Brill also tells agents to use corks that have been shaved on one side so they are "not too straight, but not too much cut off so the player notices it." Corks that have been so altered do not follow a straight line, Brill writes.

Target Joint

In this game, the player shoots at perhaps 120 rectangular targets in three sizes and three colors – white, red and green – that stand vertically on narrow shelves. This is a game where the player typically keeps shooting until he or she wins. Almost inevitably, the player wins a prize such as a pocket comb. The player stands about seven feet from the shelves.

All targets are made from two pieces of wood 2 inches wide by ¼-inch thick. The white target – the one worth the most valuable prize – is 4 inches tall and attached to a 4-inch-long base. However, the vertical target is attached 1 inch from one end of the base. The short end of the base is turned toward the player, so the cork must have enough energy to power over 3 inches of the base at the back of the target. This is highly unlikely.

The red target is 5 inches tall, with a base made exactly the same as the one described earlier.

The green target is 6 inches tall, attached to a base that is 2 inches long only in front. The green target has no back lip to prevent it from being tipped over.

To further stack the odds in his or her favor, the operator puts out more green targets than white and red targets combined. In a game observed at a county fair, there were 30 green targets, 14 white targets and 14 red targets. Green targets flank both sides of every white and red target.

Cup Joints are games of chance because players do not know the location of cups worth medium or choice prizes. The cups resting on the bottom two shelves of this game were easier to knock off because the shelves were not level.

The player naturally shoots for the white or red targets, sometimes jarring them with a strike. But since corks do not follow perfectly straight paths, one inevitably strays from its intended course and strikes a green target, which falls over easily.

Carnival investigator Riedthaler reports that some operators gaff a game by attaching the prizes themselves to the targets. In one case, he found that the cotton in the bottom of an all-metal cigarette lighter has been replaced with 1½ ounces of lead, so the target could not be tipped.

Cup Joint

In this game, the targets are 12-ounce or larger paper cups set with their mouths down on long shelves. On the bottoms of the cups are written S, M, or L, signifying whether the cup is worth a small, medium or large prize.

Some Cup Joints are run so that the carnivalgoer keeps shooting until he or she knocks a cup off the shelf. The operator then shows the bottom of the cup to the player. Other games have a specified number of shots for $1, and the player may not win any prize if he or she hasn't knocked a cup from the shelf.

Riedthaler says that operators tend to place the M or L cups on the outside edges of the shelves, which may hold a total of 120 cups in some games. Players tend to shoot at the center targets.

In a game observed by the author, the lower shelves were all tilted downward away from the player, while cups on the two upper shelves were level. Cups on the bottom shelves – which all appeared to be worth small prizes – were just about eye level for the player.

Gene Sorrows, a carny of 15 years experience who helped police identify gaffed games, says some agents operate their games so that all the cups on the shelves have an S mark. If anyone questions whether the game is gaffed, the carny just knocks a few of the cups off the shelf into a trough below and produces an M or L cup that was there previously.

Sorrows says there may be a similar arrangement when the game is played with targets of pingpong balls resting atop soda bottles.

Cigarette Joints

This game has been on the midway since the turn of the century, and it is still going strong. The object of the game is to win a pack of cigarettes or a similar-sized target by knocking it off the shelf or stand within a limited number of shots, usually three for $1. Targets that fall forward from the shelves are not counted as winners.

Shelves can range in width from 4 to 6 inches, and operators control which items can be won by their positions on the shelf. Valuable targets are set near the front edge of the shelves so they will tend to lie down if they are struck, rather than fall off the back edge of the shelf.

The best way to win is to hit the pack of cigarettes directly in its center, Riedthaler says.

Between the packs of cigarettes are empty boxes of matches, which are a cinch to knock off the shelf. What often happens is this: A player aims for a cigarette pack, the shot strays from the intended target, and the cork knocks off a match box – ending the game. Players are given a full box of matches for knocking off an empty box.

Brill suggests that carnies also should use "circus candy" as prizes along with cigarette packs. Circus candy is extremely cheap confections contained in a relatively large box. While the boxes of candy look impressive, they cost only pennies.

Riedthaler says some games use targets that are blocks of wood larger than a cigarette pack and are worth a choice prize; but these wooden targets tend to be too heavy and long to be knocked off the shelf by a flying cork. Sorrows reports it is also futile to shoot at a pack of cigarettes enclosed in a clear plastic case. The case has too much inertia to be moved by the cork.

Riedthaler reports that some unscrupulous operators glue a strip of rough grade sandpaper all along the back of the shelf to stop any cigarette pack from going over the back edge. Other grifters have the back canvas covering so close to the shelf that there isn't enough space to allow a cigarette pack to fall, he says.

Carnies aren't the only ones who cheat at cork galleries. Brill warns carnies against "sharpers," or experienced players, who replace the cork in the gun barrel with a cork that has a roofing nail or heavy tack inserted in its center. With the added weight, the corks easily knock cigarette packs off their pedestals.

Chapter 13

Cat Rack

If you are not fond of cats, this is the game for you. If you are, skip this chapter.

The object of Cat Rack, also known as Punk Rack or Gaucho Rack, is to throw a baseball at stuffed figures of cats, either knocking them over or off their shelves, depending on how the game is played. Drop three cats with three pitches, and take home a prize.

The game can have as many as 80 small cats lined up on several shelves at the back of the joint. A board about 3 inches wide covers the base of the cats, so a ball cannot knock the stuffed animals off the shelf by hitting their feet.

The targets are stuffed animals 11 to 12 inches high, 5 inches at their widest point, and edged with about 1½ inches of fake fur to give them the appearance of being larger. The cats usually rest on wooden bases with leather edges.

Players stand 12 to 22 feet from the target when they pitch at the punks. The balls can be anything from regulation, leather-covered baseballs to specially made carnival balls with sawdust centers.

The Secret

Carnival consultant Snyder says Punk Rack is essentially a game that depends on a person's skill at throwing a baseball, and is not commonly gaffed. Some people miss the cats entirely, and a good number hit the 3-inch board that covers the base of the cats, Snyder says.

Although it appears to be heavy, a punk used in Punk Rack usually can be knocked over with a soft but accurate toss.

Players throw from about 12 feet in a typical Punk Rack setup.

Carnival investigator Riedthaler says the best technique is simply to toss the ball – even the lightweight variety – so it strikes the punk directly. No need to go through a windup to hurl the ball, he says.

"Everyone thinks the cat weighs 200 pounds," he says. "And then they throw so hard they beat themselves." A punk is made from two pieces of canvas sewn together and stuffed with rags, so it weighs only about two-thirds of a pound.

One carny who operated a Punk Rack says the best place to strike a punk is right in the head. The throw exerts its greatest leverage there, he says.

The joint he operated had about 60 punks, and players made their throws from 12 feet with regulation, leather-covered balls.

Although the game was not clocked for the odds at winning, it was obvious that people could win if they had some skill at throwing a ball. Many people missed because they threw the ball too hard.

The operator figured that he gave out about $5 in stock for every $12 taken in.

Words of Caution

Former carny Sorrows warns that Punk Rack is a traditional game for a build-up. For example, the agent offers to make one out of three shots for a carnivalgoer so that he continues to play – and pay. If an agent makes such an offer, decline and play another game. It is a sure sign that the agent is working the game "strong" and is out to take the player for money.

Riedthaler says the game can be gaffed in various ways. The easiest way is with the use of a pinch board – a thin rail attached to the back of the shelf and hidden from the player's sight by the front board.

The agent places the stuffed cat between the front board and the rail and gives the base of the cat a quarter turn, wedging the cat between the boards. This prevents a cat from being knocked over.

Another method is for the cat to be attached to one end of a long base. The cat can be knocked over easily or with great difficulty, depending on which way the two-sided cat is facing the player. This technique also is used in Six Cat, which is described elsewhere in this book.

Players who suspect a Punk Rack is gaffed should ask to see the punk base.

Chapter 14

Bushel Basket

This is another of the traditional midway games that arose from the time when carnivals were largely rural affairs.

The object of Bushel Basket or Peach Basket is to toss one or two softballs from a distance of about six feet into a bushel basket fixed at an angle on a board with legs. The bottom of the basket has a lot of spring to it, largely due to the way it is connected to the baseboard.

When the game is played legitimately, Bushel Basket presents the public with a fair chance of winning a large prize.

However, players should inspect the equipment and ask about all rules of the game before handing over their money. Bushel Basket can be gaffed easily and quickly so that the public has little chance of winning.

Sometimes agents use specially made carnival balls that can weigh as little as 4 ounces, rather than the 6¼-ounce minimum weight of an official softball. The lighter ball makes the game harder to win.

The Secret

The chances of winning depend on the player's skill in placing the ball on a part of the basket that will absorb most of the ball's energy. The best throw is to have the ball drop in from a high arc, so that it enters the basket from a vertical angle rather than a horizontal angle.

The player should aim for the lip or the sides of the basket. However, the player should find out first whether either or both of these

Bushel Basket is largely a game of skill, but watch out for alibi agents.

shots are against the rules of the game. If both shots are forbidden, it will be a tough game to win.

Questions to ask include: Where is the foul line? How far can a player lean in before he is over the line? Are rim shots legal and what is considered a rim shot? Can the player make shots from the side or hit the sides of the basket?

Thoroughly understand the rules before playing, and then decide whether the game is just too hard to win.

The worst place to put the ball is directly on the bottom of the basket. Since every other slat of the bottom of the basket is nailed or screwed to the baseboard, the bottom of the basket has a lot of natural spring that will immediately eject a ball tossed upon it.

Also take note how far from plumb the basket leans. The closer the angle of the basket to vertical, the harder it will be for the ball to remain in the basket. Carnival consultant Snyder says a change of only 2 degrees in angle can make a great difference in the number of winners.

Carnival equipment supplier Dawson says an operator can throw about 25 percent stock if he or she sets the basket at a 45 degree angle, throws are made from about six feet and the arc of the ball is not hindered by hanging prizes.

In a Bushel Basket game observed at a state fair in summer 1987, 15 wins occurred in 1,002 tosses – a winner had to make both shots to win. It cost $1 for two balls, and the prize was a 20-foot stuffed snake that Acme Premium sold wholesale that year for about $24.

Under those circumstances, the payout in prizes was nearly 72 percent of the gross receipts – a very high percentage in favor of the players.

The manager of the game said there probably was a lucky streak during clocking of the game. He said the average payout was closer to about 30 percent of the gross receipts.

Shots were made with an Acme Premium "Official Soft Ball," weighing 5 ounces, from a distance of about six feet. Rim shots were allowed, but side shots were not. The bushel baskets were ordinary baskets made by the Little Rock Crate & Basket Co., Little Rock, Ark., and the baskets were attached to a solid flat backboard.

Words of Caution

Before playing, check the type of ball being used. Some unscrupulous carnies will use a heavier ball when demonstrating how the game works, or give players a heavier ball for a practice shot; then, when play begins, they substitute a lighter ball that is harder to keep in the basket. Ask to use the same ball the carny used for all your actual shots.

The agent may demonstrate how easy the game is to win by deftl tossing both balls into the basket from where he or she is standing i the booth. But in this situation, too, the agent has advantages ove the player.

First, the agent makes his throws from the side of the basket rathe than directly in front of it. That means the ball depletes its energy o the side of the basket instead of its rather springy bottom.

The second advantage is that the agent leaves the first ball in th basket when he makes his second shot. The first ball deadens th velocity of the second ball as it enters the basket.

And third, the agent usually is throwing a shorter distance.

Bushel Basket also is a game often operated by an alibi agent – a agent who nullifies a win by telling the player he broke some rule o the game. Snyder says the best way for players to get around this is t have the agent explain all the rules before they hand over any money

The agent's favorite alibis for calling a win void are: leaning ove the foul line when making the throw, and hitting a rim shot whe rim shots aren't allowed. Know before you play what will be consid ered illegal, and play by the rules.

Carnival investigator Riedthaler says some carnies also add extr spring to the bottom of the baskets by secreting sponges underneat the slats.

Chapter 15

Break a Plate

These games appeal to the kid in us who gleefully wants to see things smashed. No need to follow complicated rules here. The object is to hurl a baseball hard enough and straight enough to chip plates and records or shatter beer bottles held in a stand.

In the short-throw version of Break a Plate, players pitch from a point about seven feet away from a rack holding plates 6½ inches in diameter and made of unglazed bisqueware or a breakable plastic material. This game generally uses regulation baseballs with leather covers.

The plates are held between 2-by-4s fastened together with metal building cleats. A chiseled-out section holds the plates so they are secure but can be turned if there is only a minor chip. The smallest space between two plates is 2⅜ inches. But the player must chip two plates at the same time to win, so the game certainly is no cake walk to win.

The backboard is made of sheet metal painted flat black.

In the long-throw version of Break a Record, the player stands about 22 feet from a rack holding 78-rpm records made of Bakelite, a plastic that is very brittle and easily broken.

To win, the player must throw a ball and break one of the records, which are about 9⅞ inches in diameter. The distance from the edge of one record to the next is a little over three inches, and roughly the bottom one-third of the records is protected by the 2-by-4 stand from being hit.

In Break a Record, players attempt to chip a 78-rpm record at a distance of about 22 feet.

Players are required to chip both plates with a baseball in some versions of Break a Plate.

In one game observed, the operator was using string-covered balls that were about 9¼ inches in circumference and covered with electrical tape. The operator of the game said the balls' leather covers had been torn off by the jagged edges of the broken records, so tape was used to repair them.

The game was not checked for the average number of wins vs. attempts, but several people won stuffed animals that wholesaled for about $1.50 each. Although the balls varied in weight, they all seemed heavy enough to break the records easily.

No side-angle or cross-arm throws are allowed, and there usually is a one-prize limit.

To win Break a Bottle, the player generally must break two bottles in two throws for $1. The targets normally are long-neck beer bottles placed about four inches from each other in racks made up of 2-by-4s. Throws generally are made from a distance of about 22 feet.

The Secret

Carnival experts tend to agree that Break a Plate, Record or Bottle is a game of skill that depends on the throwing ability of the player. This family of games usually awards fairly nice prizes that range from $1.50 to $4.50 wholesale.

Throws in Break a Bottle are made from about 22 feet.

Since the pitching ability needed to be successful in these games is considerable, it is largely a matter of luck when the average player wins.

For instance, the plates in a short-range game are set next to each other so their closest distance is a half-inch less than the diameter of the baseball. This essentially leaves a quarter-inch of room for error in the throw – which is a pretty close tolerance for a throw from seven feet.

Carnival investigator Riedthaler says some operators place a board on the rail in front of the plates or records. Raising or lowering the board affects the size of the target. All else being equal, a player will have a better chance of winning a Break a Plate or Record game where such a board is below the halfway point.

When it comes to targets, the author believes that Break a Bottle is somewhat harder, because indirect hits tend to glance off the bottles without breaking them. Riedthaler says that, in his experience, a plate or record always chips when struck by a ball – even if the ball catches only an edge.

Chapter 16

Basketball

This game appeals, of course, to the athletes among us who have a good eye and a steady shot with a basketball. But the carnival variety of basketball can take two forms on the midway: as a hanky pank and as a true test of skill.

Some Basketball games are operated from a relatively short distance, perhaps four feet. The object of the game is simply to toss the basketball underhand into a hoop that is smaller than the 18-inch, inside diameter goal used in regulation basketball games. The player wins a prize every time he or she accomplishes this task, and players can trade smaller prizes for larger ones.

However, this is a typical hanky pank where the operator charges much more per play than the value of the prize awarded. For instance, in one game observed in the summer of 1987, players received a prize worth less than 10 cents for the $1 it cost to play. It took several wins and trade-ups before a player received a significant prize.

But other Basketball games require much more skill of the player, and consequently offer much larger prizes for $1 per play.

The Secret

There are several ways that carnies can make a midway Basketball game more difficult than, say, attempting free throws in a high school gymnasium. They can use a smaller goal or a larger ball, make the height of the net lower or higher than regulation, or draw

Basketball games, such as this one using regulation equipment, are games of skill.

the foul line farther away than a regulation free-throw line.

In most cases, the player must make both shots to win a choice prize. Operators often limit a player to one win per day.

Acme Premium Supply Corp. sells Basketball goals that have an inside diameter of 13 inches or 15 inches. It also sells a regulation goal that has been squished into an ellipse so that its minor axis is 13 inches.

The company suggests that some operators may want to simply have a welder remove a piece of a regulation metal basketball hoop. Acme Premium tells operators to draw a foul line about eight to 10 feet from the net when the smaller goals are used.

It encourages operators to post prominently a sign in 1-inch letters that states "Not Regulation Diameter" for goals that are less than 18 inches in diameter.

The game should always be played with balls that are official size and weight, Acme Premium says.

If a regulation goal is used, the foul line should be about 12 feet from the net, the company states.

Regardless of the height or distance of the goal, there should be a minimum of 1½ inches of clearance for the ball to go through the basket, and the goal should be mounted rigidly on a solid backboard of not less than ¾-inch plywood or similar material.

Carnival investigator Riedthaler says that some operators overinflate balls, so they have more bounce than a regulation ball and are tougher to get through the goal.

Operators also may not attach hoops securely to a backboard, so the rims vibrate when they are struck by the ball, Riedthaler says. That prevents rim shots from going through the net.

Chapter 17

Crazy Ball

Faced with color and pattern combinations such as rainbow blue, gaudy checks and zebra stripes, a player quickly sees why this game is called Crazy Ball.

But one aspect of this group game isn't crazy: Carnival experts say Crazy Ball presents one of the best opportunities on the midway for a person with average athletic skill to win a prize.

The object of the game is to correctly guess where a ball will land on a board riddled with 100 holes. Players put their bets on a counter called a laydown, which has 25 different colors and designs.

The typical Crazy Ball joint is in the middle of the midway, and each of its four sides has its own laydown. The playing field is in the middle of the joint and surrounded by clear plastic walls so the players can see where the ball lands.

Although manufacturers of Crazy Ball say it is a game of skill, that statement is made largely to satisfy law enforcement agents who are on the lookout for gaffed gambling devices on the midway. For all practical purposes, Crazy Ball is a game of chance, but the odds are pretty good for the average carnivalgoer.

The Secret

For a Crazy Ball game with 25 colors and 100 holes with four of each color, the probability of the player winning is one in 25.

Unless he or she wants to place more than one bet, the player's odds of winning do not change with the number of players. So a

Crazy Ball can be one of the best ways for a player with little athletic skill to win a large prize at a carnival.

player's odds don't decrease just because other people are playing too – unless the operator forbids more than one person to play a color.

The typical game in 1987 cost 25 cents for a color. A little arithmetic shows that an agent would take in $6.25 if there were 25 players in a game, and would give out a prize worth perhaps $2.50 wholesale.

To be running a layout with every color taken every time would be ideal for the agent, but that happens only occasionally. An agent often runs the game with fewer players, taking in less money and playing the odds that no one will win.

The prize is smaller than those found in games demanding a high degree of skill and costing $1 per play, but the relative odds of winning are much higher in Crazy Ball for the average individual.

Game manufacturer Hampton says a Crazy Ball operator must "buy smart" – in other words, be shrewd about the wholesale price to pay for merchandise – because the average payout for the game is about 40 percent of the gross collection.

Crazy Ball, like Duck Pond, belongs to that family of carnival games that is strictly a matter of chance. Most law enforcement agencies accept the argument that there is skill involved when the player tosses the ball into the clear plastic box, although they concede that the skill element is so small, it is inconsequential.

And gaming experts say that law enforcement agencies should "wink at" these sorts of games where many cheap prizes are given out. Games like Crazy Ball – as long as people are not playing for money – are harmless, fun, and give the average carnivalgoer a fair chance of taking home a souvenir.

Chapter 18

Wheels and Spindles

Known to the carnies simply as wheels, wheels of fortune are probably the most versatile of all carnival games and among the most entertaining. The carny has an opportunity to give out a wide variety of prizes and knows with a fair amount of accuracy how much he can afford to give out in stock.

If they are not gaffed, wheels of fortune are strictly a matter of chance for the player – one reason they are outlawed on many midways. Some carnival experts say it is unfortunate that such games are not permitted, because an ungaffed wheel gives the average player a better chance of winning a large stuffed animal than many of the so-called "skill" games on the midway.

Wheels come under a variety of names, usually chosen for the type of prize they offer or the way they are operated. There are Doll Wheels, Salami Wheels, Color Wheels, Chuck-A-Luck Wheels, Slum Wheels, Color Wheels, Rat Wheels and Horse Race Wheels, to name a few. Regardless of the name, they are all games of chance.

Basically, wheels can be broken down into wheels and spindles. A wheel spins, and there are a number of pins on its circumference that strike a stationary clicker, slowing the wheel to a stop. Wheels can be either horizontal or vertical.

Spindles are made up of a heavy arrow or pointer that rotates in the middle of a horizontal board that remains stationary. A clicker on the end of the arrow strikes pins stuck in the board.

In most cases, players place their bets on a counter in front of the

Wheels of fortune are one of the oldest games on the midway.

wheel or spindle, and the carny spins the wheel or arrow. A winner is declared when the arrow points to a chosen color or number, or when a chosen color or number comes to rest under the clicker of a wheel.

The basic game has other variations. In one game, a player picks the winning number or color by throwing a dart at a vertical wheel that is spinning, ostensibly adding some element of skill. Another favorite, the Rat Wheel, lets a rodent pick the winner. A live rat is placed in a cage or toy house in the center of a large wheel, which is then spun. Players bet on which hole the rat will take refuge in when the house is lifted. The holes, each a different color, are near the edge of the wheel.

The Secret

Wheels are strictly a game of chance, unless the equipment is gaffed. A player can determine his or her chances of winning on a simple number wheel by dividing the number of bets he or she makes by the total number of divisions on the wheel. For instance, a player who places one bet on a wheel with 20 divisions has one chance in 20 of winning. The more numbers or colors the player bets, the better his or her chances of winning.

But a player should try to calculate the value of the prize to be awarded before he or she places multiple bets. The player could bet 10 spots on a 20-division wheel and make his chance of winning 50-50.

If the bet is 50 cents a spot, the player would be betting a total of $5 for 50-50 odds. But the prize probably is worth considerably less than $5.

Here's how a carny decides what prize he or she can offer per spin. In the game just described, the carny could gross $10 on a spin where every number was bet.

The carny decides on a percentage payout for a prize per spin, perhaps 25 percent of gross, or $2.50 in this example. So the player who bet $5 on half of the spots on the wheel may receive a prize that normally would cost him or her $2.50 – and that's if he or she wins.

In actuality, a prize worth $2.50 to the player may have cost the carny less, because the carny purchases stock wholesale. But in all fairness, a carnival cannot be likened to a local store. The player receives a prize that essentially cannot be purchased by everybody, and also gets the entertainment value of having won a prize at a carnival. That excitement cannot be bought in any store.

Odd as it may sound, the carny's probability of winning doesn't change if only a few people bet or if more than one person bets on a particular color or number.

This Spindle is gaffed so the operator can make the arrow stop on black or white simply by pushing a button.

Words of Caution

Wheels and spindles have a long history of being gaffed, going back in America at least to the Civil War.

Law enforcement agencies say wheels are often gaffed to give the agent control over where the arrow or wheel stops. When an unscrupulous agent notices that there is heavy betting on a particular number or color, he makes sure the wheel stops elsewhere.

Carnival investigator Riedthaler says there are some indications when a wheel is gaffed. On a vertical or horizontal wheel, the player should observe whether the axle on which the wheel turns also moves. If the center post turns, there may be a hidden brake that can be applied to the wheel to stop its spin on a particular number or color.

Another indication of gaffing is when the clicker is made from a pliable material, such as leather, that doesn't make much noise while the wheel is spinning. In this case, the agent can apply the brake to the wheel without causing abrupt stops that would arouse suspicion.

Some brakes are controlled by the wheel agent himself, while other brakes can be controlled in the joint next door. The wheel agent can alert his confederate next door that the wheel should be stopped by calling out a phrase.

Walter B. Gibson, in his book describing carnival games prevalent on midways in the late 1920s, reports that a wheel gaff may be as simple as a thumbtack with a piece of lead soldered to it. The thumbtack is positioned at the back of the wheel opposite the number that is to "win." Vertical wheels also can be rigged with an electromagnet that slows the wheel and finally stops it on a selected number.

The Rat Wheel described earlier in this chapter can be gaffed with the use of a little ammonia, according to plans for carnival games published by A.K. Brill.

When running a gaffed Rat Wheel, the agent observes which numbers or colors are not bet. Brill advises that "if the operator will dip finger in ammonia (can be diluted with water) and rub finger around hole in color on which least money is played – mouse will run to that hole, attracted by ammonia odor, and percentage of profit will be increased. The ammonia should be wiped from hole of previous play. Do it unobtrusively."

In a 1912 book on gambling, John Philip Quinn describes several techniques for rigging wheels and spindles that are still in use today. One general technique is to build the stand of a wheel with a metal rod in its middle, unseen by players. When the agent wants to stop the wheel on a particular number, he or she applies pressure on the rod, which then rubs against the axle on which the wheel turns.

In a spindle developed in the 1860s, Quinn says, the agent could stop the arrow on a certain number or color just by applying pressure on a leg of the solid-metal tripod on which the arrow spun.

Riedthaler says some carnies use a "belly gaff" on a spindle to control the outcome of the game. A plastic clicker on the tip of the arrow brushes a number of thin flat metal strips that have been twisted and set on the perimeter of the circle.

Players try to guess the number or color on which the arrow will come to rest. Riedthaler says a typical number game may have 48 numbers or colors, with a stop every 7½ degrees around the circle.

Unknown to the players, the carny can make the clicker – which normally rests at an angle – become vertical whenever he pushes a hidden button. When the clicker is vertical, it brushes against only certain parts of the twisted metal strips. So the carny can control the color on which the arrow stops or whether the number will be odd or even.

Riedthaler says this particular game has a variation in which the arrow can be made to stop on sections marked for small, medium or large prizes. Half of the 48 sections are marked small, one-quarter are marked medium, and the remaining quarter are large.

When the game is run normally, the clicker will stop only at small-prize sections, which get the winning player slum worth only pennies. However, the carny can cause someone to win a medium prize

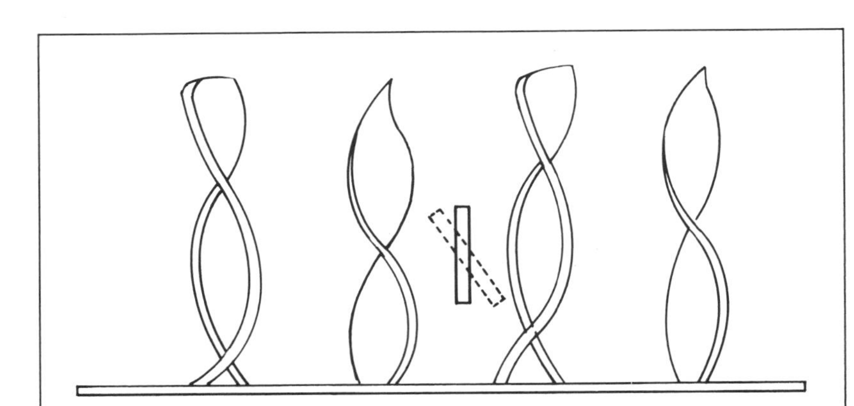

The clicker on one type of gaffed spindle turns slightly from vertical, so the clicker will not brush against some pegs (upper diagram). Another gaffed spindle has a clicker that moves up or down, insuring that some prizes cannot be won (lower diagram).

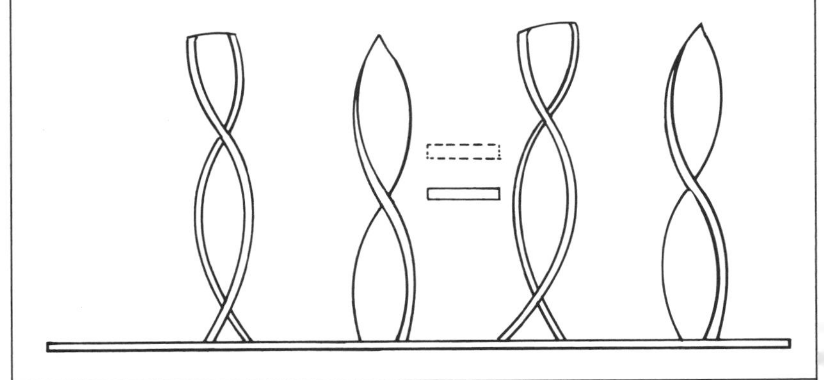

by pushing slightly on a hidden button that raises the arrow a fraction, perhaps $^{1}/_{32}$nd of an inch. The clicker then brushes against only the medium-prize sections. By leaning hard on the hidden button, the carny can raise the arrow another fraction of an inch and cause the clicker to brush against only the large-prize sections.

To show the tip that the game is not rigged so that only small prizes are won, the carny sometimes may allow a player, or a confederate, to win a medium or large prize.

Chapter 19

Bean Bag

Here's a fun game for those sporting carnivalgoers who believe they have good pitching arms. The object of Bean Bag is to knock six cans entirely off a platform with two throws with a bean bag. The cans – usually weighted with liquid plastic, paraffin or rosin – are stacked like a pyramid for the men and in a square for the women.

It is a game based on the throwing skill of the player, but law enforcement agents say that cans the carnies use have as much as 6 ounces of weight at their bottoms. That means the player has to land two well-placed throws to topple the cans with bean bags that may weigh only 3½ ounces.

The Secret

Well-placed throws are the secret to Bean Bag, also known as Knock Over the Can. The bags should hit the top of the rectangle of space where three cans meet. Players who practice have better chances of winning.

Carnival consultant Snyder says Knock Over the Can games on the midway generally are operated as hanky panks for the kids. He says he has never found a Bean Bag to be gaffed, although operators who want to cut down on the number of prizes they award usually move the cans farther back.

A carny who operated a Bean Bag said the game can be gaffed by placing cans with their weighted sides up on the upper level of the stack. When a bean bag strikes the middle of the stack, the upper-

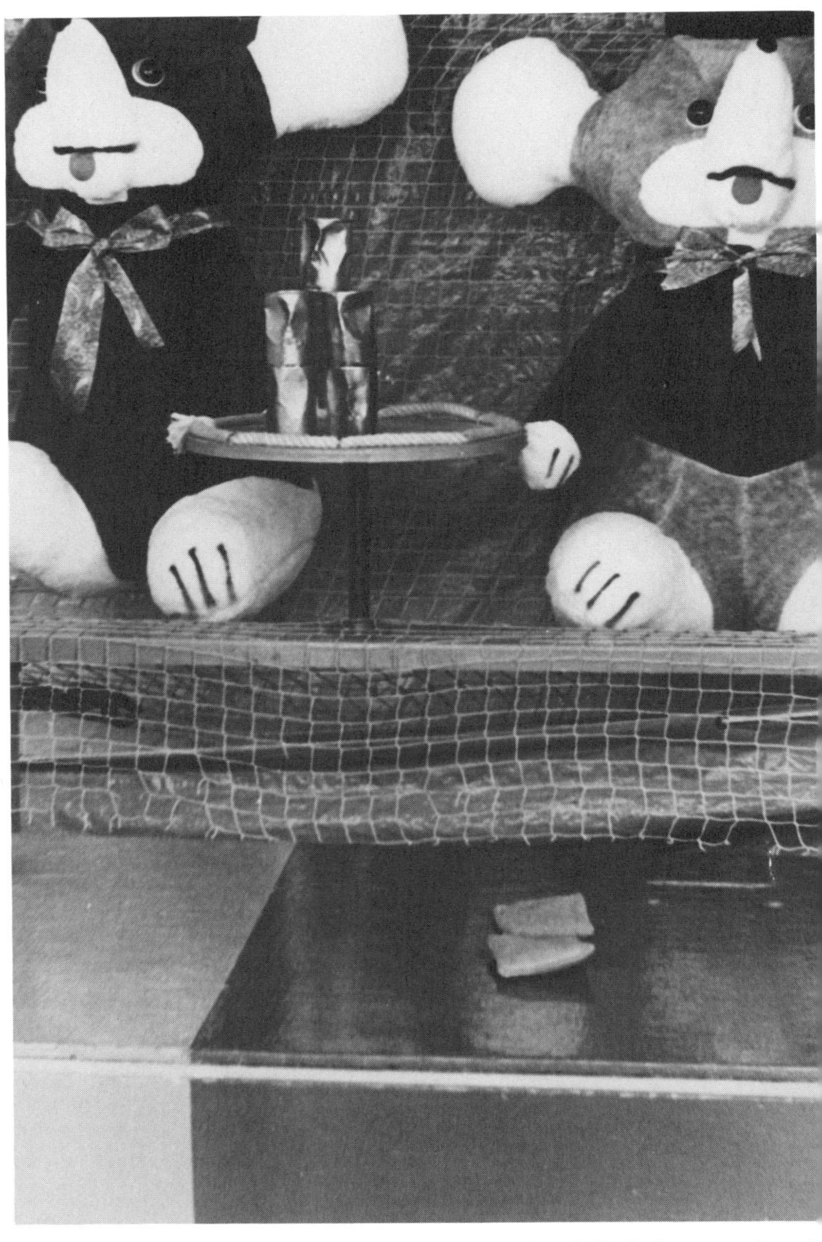

Bean Bag, a common midway game, relies on the skill of players to knock the cans off the pedestal.

level cans drop straight down on the stand because of the way their weight is distributed. But she said the game is rarely run this way since it operates normally as a hanky pank.

In the particular game she operated, the cans had about an inch of liquid plastic in their bottoms. The cans could be knocked off the stand fairly easily if the throw was correctly placed.

Acme Premium Supply Corp., which sells equipment for Bean Bag, suggests to operators that the cans be empty, and that bean bags measure about 4 inches square and weigh at least 3¼ ounces. The author believes that most cans used on the midway, however, usually are weighted.

A circular platform for the cans should not be more than 18 inches in diameter, and a square platform should not have sides more than 18 inches long, the company says.

Tom Dawson, chairman of Acme Premium, says the spacing between the cans is one way to control the difficulty of the game. A carny who wants to make the game harder to win will space the cans farther apart.

Acme Premium suggests that cans should be no farther apart than three-eighths of an inch.

How to Build Your Own Game

The materials for a basic Bean Bag game can be found around the house, the supermarket and the hobby shop. Materials and tools needed: hammer; needles and thread; six soda or soup cans all the same size (small Campbell's soup cans 2⅝ inches in diameter and 4 inches tall are a good size); plastic casting resin and catalyst; four pieces of heavy cloth (such as denim), each 4 inches square; a package of dried navy beans or rice; a piece of plywood any thickness but at least 18 inches square; a 5-foot piece of ½-inch rope, and wire staples used for electrical cable.

Make two openings in the tops of the cans with a can opener, and remove the contents. Steel soda cans are easier to empty than soup cans, but they tend to be harder to find. Don't use aluminum soda cans.

Steel soup cans are more durable, but it is more troublesome to remove their contents. Wash out the cans thoroughly and remove their labels.

From a hobby shop or hardware store, purchase a pint of casting resin and catalyst. Following the directions on the package, thoroughly mix all the resin with the appropriate amount of catalyst and pour equal amounts into all six cans. The fumes from casting resin are acrid, so it may be best to do this procedure outside the house, or

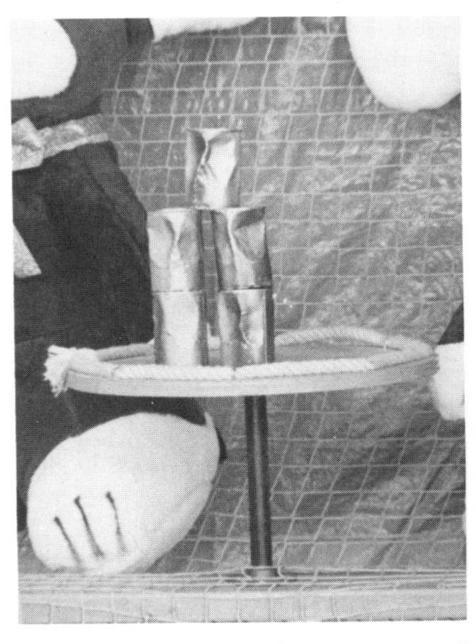

(Left): The setup for men.

(Right): The setup for women and children.

in a well-ventilated area.

When finished, the cans each weigh about 4½ ounces.

To make a bean bag, sew two of the 4-inch squares together on three sides. Turn the material inside out and fill the bag with as many beans or as much rice as will fit, leaving enough material to sew the fourth side securely. Make the second bag the same way. These bags will have an average weight of 4 ounces.

Find the center of the sheet of plywood and draw a circle 18 inches in diameter. If you don't have a compass that opens up far enough to draw the circle, push a thumbtack or pushpin into the center of the board and loop a piece of string about 20 inches long around it. Hold the ends of the string taut with one hand, measure 9 inches from the thumbtack along the strings, and mark both pieces of string at that point. Tie the ends of the strings together at the marks, and place the tip of a pencil or pen in the loop. Draw a circle using the taut loop as a guide.

Place the rope around the perimeter of the circle and fasten it to the board with the staples. The rope prevents the cans from rolling off the game board when they are knocked down but not out of the circle.

To play the game, set the cans on the game board in the pyramid fashion shown in the photographs, and stand about six feet away. The game should be positioned about waist high. The object of the game is to clear all the cans from the circle with two throws of the bean bags.

A more elaborate Bean Bag that more closely approximates a real-life carnival game can be built by cutting out the wooden circle with a saber or jigsaw before the rope is attached, and placing it on a stand.

With the thumbtack point as your guide, use wood screws to attach a pipe flange to one side of the wooden circle. Obtain a piece of pipe about 2½ feet long with threads on one end that screw into the flange.

To make the foot of the stand, get two pieces of 2-by-4 that are 24 inches long and cut out squares halfway through the boards at their midpoints. Fit the pieces together and drill a hole for the pipe halfway into the boards. If the foot is wobbly, hammer a thin piece of wood into the crack where the two boards meet.

Paint gives the entire game a finished appearance. It is best to put some sort of barrier, such as an old blanket or net, around three sides of the game to catch the cans and beans bags.

Chapter 20

One Ball

The popular game of One Ball or Spill the Milk appeals most to baseball fans, Little Leaguers and weekend softball players. The game sometimes is a true test of skill, and sometimes it is impossible to win.

If it is run legitimately, Spill the Milk is relatively difficult to win.

The object of One Ball is to knock down a pyramid composed of three aluminum bottles about 8 inches tall that are shaped like the old-fashioned, glass containers that held a quart of milk.

The bottles – weighted at the bottom with one to three pounds of lead, if the game is legitimate – are set with two on the bottom touching and the third on the top. The bottles are set on a table perhaps 18 inches high.

The game requires a player to knock the bottles not only down but off the table in one throw. The player usually is given a regulation softball for the task, and he makes the pitch from a point about seven feet away from the table.

The Secret

Carnies say the best way to win at One Ball is a direct hit in the triangular area where the three bottles meet. That is easier said than done.

One carny conceded that he could bring the bottles down successfully only about three times out of 10 tries – and he had practiced. Another carny said children generally are more successful at One

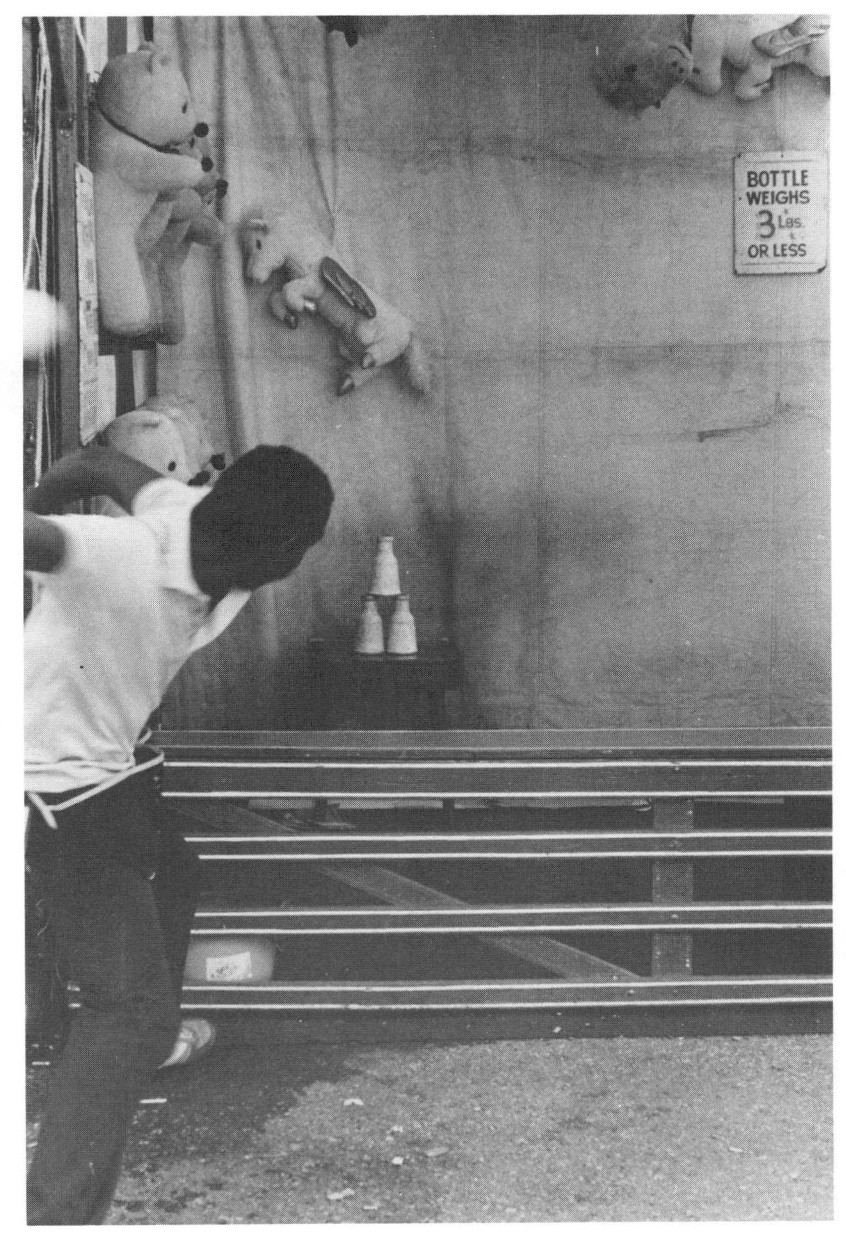

Carnies say the ideal target in Spill the Milk is the triangle formed where the three bottles meet.

Ball because they view the target near eye level, while adults must throw the ball at a downward angle.

At an observation of a Spill the Milk game being run at a state fair in 1987, there was only one winner out of 472 trials, and the sole winner cheated. The cheater caught a rebound from his first throw and knocked down the remaining bottle when the carny wasn't looking.

In the game observed, players paid $1 a turn to throw leather-covered softballs 12 inches in circumference and weighing 6 ounces, about the weight of an official ball. The operator conceded that the bottles weighed more than three pounds, but would not give the exact weights or answer other questions about the game.

Acme Premium Supply Corp., which sells equipment for One Ball, suggests to operators that they set the bottles on a low stand, such as a soda bottle case, and have players throw from a distance of eight to 10 feet. Acme sells cast aluminum bottles in one- and three-pound weights.

In places where the setup is not illegal, Acme advises operators to use one heavy bottle and two light ones.

The company also is proposing game standards that state no bottle may weigh over six pounds, and balls must be a minimum of 6 ounces in weight. Those standards forbid the use of a rim around the table if all bottles must be knocked entirely off.

Players who have good arms and want to try their luck at One Ball should ask before they hand over their money exactly what sort of equipment they will use. Ask about the weights of the bottles and the ball, and don't play until you get a satisfactory answer. Ask to examine the bottles and observe whether they are all the same weight or whether the weight is distributed in each bottle unevenly.

Check to see if the weights in the bottles can slide. If the weight slides, a carny, with a simple flip of the wrist, can gaff the game to make it impossible to win.

Finally, observe whether all the bottles are flush with each other and with the player – as they should be if the game is being played fairly.

Words of Caution

Former carny Sorrows called One Ball perhaps the most controversial game on the midway, because a good number of them are run in what he says is a "shady fashion." Sorrows says dishonest agents will set one heavier bottle on the bottom row and slightly to the rear. That way, the ball will hit the lighter two bottles first, and won't have enough energy to carry the heavier bottle off.

Some unscrupulous operators plug the hole in the bottom of the aluminum bottle with a broomstick and add molten lead (right) so the bottle is too heavy to be knocked over with a softball. Other operators cast lead on the side of the bottle so it can be knocked down – but not off – the stand (left).

When a carny wants to show that the game can be won, he puts the heavy bottle on the top of the pyramid.

Carnival investigator Riedthaler says there may be a different setup when the player is allowed two shots. One bottle may be unweighted, with the remaining two having different weights. The carny sets the unweighted bottle on top, and gives the player a softball that carries a little extra weight. If the player strikes the center of the pyramid, the top bottle flies off, the lighter lower bottle is knocked over, and the heavier bottle remains standing.

The player is then given an ultralight ball that cannot be thrown hard enough to knock over the heavier bottle.

Chapter 21

Dip Bowl

The Dip Bowl or Bowler Roller game has become much more common on the midway in the past decade, and for good reason. It can be played by people of all ages, yet it is a challenging game.

It costs a nominal amount to play Bowler Roller. Usually, a quarter inserted into a coin box activates the game. Although the prizes tend to be small, the chances of the player winning are good compared with other carnival games described in this book. Most operators offer to take back smaller prizes in trade for one larger.

Dip Bowl is played with a regulation bowling ball and a track about 8 feet long that is level for the first half of its length, followed by a crest and a trough. When a coin is inserted in the game slot, an arm that holds the ball partway up the track falls so the ball can roll into the hands of the customer.

The object of the game is to give the bowling ball just enough push to make it travel over the crest and come to rest in the trough.

What commonly happens is that players give the ball too much push and it travels over the crest, gathers momentum in the trough, hits a bumper at the end of the game, makes a return trip and is caught by the arm. The player then usually overcompensates by not giving the ball enough push to top the crest, and again it returns and is caught by the arm.

There is plenty of carnival "flash" when a player successfully wins Bowler Roller. When a ball rests in the trough, it pushes down a pneumatic switch that activates a flasher and siren.

Bowler Roller requires a deft touch to give the ball enough energy to top the crest, but not enough push so the ball returns.

The Secret

Dip Bowl or Bowler Roller primarily is a game of skill, and the question becomes how many times a player is willing to lose to acquire the necessary skill.

John Mendes Jr., general manager of Bob's Space Racers Inc., estimated that it may take the average person between 10 and 12 tries before he is successful at the game. Bob's Space Racers, one of the nation's largest makers of custom-designed carnival games, manufactures and sells Bowler Roller.

June Hardin, president of Wapello Fabrications Inc. in Wapello, Iowa, says the game can be won consistently after it is practiced. She says her sons, who help construct the Dip Bowl games sold by Wapello, can win the game regularly. But she conceded that it is really a matter of luck for the average person to walk up and win without practice.

During observation of a Bowler Roller game operating at a state fair in 1987, a total of 497 attempts to roll the ball in the trough resulted in 15 wins. A prize worth under perhaps 20 cents wholesale was awarded on the first win, but players who progressively got better walked away with much better prizes when they traded up.

Customers should ask before playing the game what prize is awarded for the first win. First-win prizes usually are very small toys kept in a nearby bin or under the counter, while larger, stuffed animals are displayed prominently.

First-win prizes certainly are not worth $3, the amount it would cost the average player paying 25 cents per game for a dozen games. But then, a player should ask himself whether the entertainment value of playing Dip Bowl isn't worth the money.

Chapter 22

Duck Pond Catch the Can

Duck Pond, a game in which players snatch plastic ducks from a flock floating in a metal trough filled with circulating water, has been a favorite with children for decades.

Duck Pond and its cousin, Fish Pond, are strictly games of chance.

However, Catch the Can is a game of skill. Anyone who plays the game – usually adults – will find adequate challenge of his or her ability to "hook" a small red disc swirling among many discs in a trough of water.

Duck or Fish Pond

There was a public outcry when Michael Mihm decided the Duck Pond game could not be run at the Heart of Illinois Fair in 1973 because it constituted an illegal lottery. Mihm, state attorney general at the time and now a federal judge in Peoria, Ill., was considered a spoilsport by some.

A local newspaper started a story about Mihm's campaign with the headline "There Goes Molly's Rubber Ducky Game," in reference to Mihm's then 4-year-old daughter, who loved to play Duck Pond.

Mihm himself conceded that he liked to play carnival games, and said the stance against Duck Ponds and some other games made him feel "uncomfortable." He later allowed the game on the midway with one alteration from the way it was normally played. Mirrors were placed in the bottom of the trough so players could see the numbers on the bottoms of the ducks floating by.

Duck Pond is operated as a hanky pank, where every player wins a prize.

Mihm said it was unlikely that the mirrors seriously changed the manner in which people played – children still just grabbed their favorite colors – but the mirrors added an element of skill that made the game legal.

The story of Mihm and the rubber ducky illustrates two things about Duck Pond: It is essentially a game of chance, and it is popular with the public, particularly parents with small children.

So it is one of those carnival games – like Crazy Ball – that law enforcement officials tend to wink at, even though it is a game of chance. As long as the price to play and the prizes are small, a carnivalgoer has little chance of being cheated. It is only when valuable goods are offered as prizes that the players should beware of the game.

Duck Pond generally is a hanky pank – that is, the carny wins regardless of what number the player picks. Almost all the prizes are worth pennies each, compared with the 50 cents to $1 it costs to play; and the carny makes his or her living on volume of customers.

The game has been around at least since the turn of the century, usually as Fish Pond. Unlike the way the game is played today, the early games offered valuable prizes and consequently were rigged. Players using lines and poles attempted to win the choice prizes by hooking wooden fish that had large rings in their mouths. The fish sometimes were floating in a large tub, forerunner to today's channel of circulating water.

By the early 1900s, carnies already had devised a couple of ways to cheat players. One way was to "thumb the number," or obscure a part of a number so it appeared to be a losing rather than a winning number. For instance, a carny would place his thumb over the top of the number "17" so it looked like the number "11."

Some rigged games used metal slides in place of the thumbing sleight. Instead of thumbing the number, the carny would move the slide over to obscure winners.

Modern-day Duck Ponds have plastic ducks with S, M, L or numbers marked on their bellies to signify what type of prize they will bring. Carnival investigator Riedthaler found that, on the average, there was about one duck with a number or letter winning a choice prize for every 75 ducks in the pond. The remaining ducks were worth small prizes.

The Kansas Bureau of Investigation reports that some shady operators put magnets on the bellies of large-prize ducks so they can be attached inside the metal hood that covers part of the pond – effectively taking them out of play. If a law enforcement agent stops the game for an examination, the agent merely has to rap his fingers on the top of the hood to dislodge any magnetized ducks.

However, the vast majority of Duck Ponds found at an average carnival are run legitimately as hanky panks in which everyone wins a prize. The carny makes money by offering prizes that are worth less than the cost of play, and the carnivalgoer receives the entertainment value of playing and a souvenir to boot. Duck Pond should be approached strictly as a fun game. Those who play it with the idea of winning a big prize would be better served by playing a game that requires skill.

Catch the Can

A typical Catch the Can game is played with a 58-inch-long fiberglass pole that has a string about 60 inches long attached to its end. On the other end of the string is a strong magnet capable of holding any of the discs circulating in the water trough.

One version of the game uses two sizes of discs, a plastic-coated, yellow disc about 10 inches in circumference and a smaller, red wooden or plastic disc about 5½ inches in circumference. In another version, all the discs are the same size but the prize discs are red.

The object of the game is to "hook" a prize disc with the magnet without attracting the larger, slower-moving discs. The player loses if he picks up a yellow disc or two discs.

Catch the Can, although a version of Duck Pond, is a challenge for any adult player.

Tom Dawson, who sells equipment for Catch the Can, says the difficulty of the game depends on two variables: the number of losing discs in relation to the prize discs, and the speed of the circulating water.

He says the game is very hard to win if there are more than seven times as many losing discs as prize discs. A large losing disc is made entirely of metal, while the only metal a prize disc contains is a piece of iron soda can about ½-inch square.

The best strategy is to be patient, stay still and wait for the prize discs to float by, rather than try to follow a disc with the pole. Players soon learn that the magnet – weighing several ounces – acts as a heavy sinker on the flexible pole, so just about any quick movement makes the magnet bob.

When the prize disc floats by, merely dip the arms slightly. If the arms are dropped too far, the magnet pushes the disc beneath the swirling water, which carries it away.

Prizes awarded in Catch the Can games usually are not huge stuffed animals, but some noted in 1987 were worth perhaps $1.50 to $2 wholesale. The cost to play was $1.

Chapter 23

Milk Can

A midway just isn't a midway if it doesn't have a Milk Can game, probably one of the oldest tests of skill one can find at a modern-day carnival.

Usually located in the center of the midway, the Milk Can game is in strong contrast to the growing number of mechanized and electronic games that rely on gimmicks, lights and loudspeakers.

The object of the Milk Can game is simply to toss a softball into a 10-gallon metal milk can, the kind dairies use to transport milk. But most carnival cans are not the ordinary dairy cans. For the midway game, a concave piece of steel is welded to the rim of the can's opening, reducing the size of the hole the ball must travel through to anything from 6½ inches in diameter to under 4⅜ inches in diameter.

The player usually stands four to six feet from the can, which is positioned so the lip is lower than eye level.

The Secret

Although the opening of the can may be only 1/16th of an inch larger than the diameter of the softball, carnies say the game can be won with a proper throw. They say the best way to win at the Milk Can game is to give the ball a backspin and attempt to hit the back edge of the can.

However, it takes quite a bit of practice to learn to put a backspin on the ball and still throw it accurately. Most people observed winning

Tossing a softball into a milk can with a reduced neck opening takes an accurate throw, but it can be done.

this game did so by tossing the ball directly into the hole.

There is no harm in asking the agent to show you the size of the opening before you hand over your dollar. That way, you can rest assured the game is played honestly, and you get a feel for the size of the target.

The second tip carnies offer about winning is: put as much arc on the ball as possible. Operators hang the plush prizes from the rafters of the joint, so there may be small clearance for the ball. Pick and choose which way to place a throw into a can.

At one Milk Can game played at a state fair in 1987, there were 15 wins out of a total of 1,279 tries, or one win out of about every 86 balls thrown.

The balls were 8-ounce, rubber-coated softballs that were 12 inches in circumference, and throws were made from a distance of about four feet. The prize in every case was a medium-sized Spuds MacKenzie stuffed dog that wholesaled for about $8.

Words of Caution

Carnival consultant Snyder says the Milk Can game is difficult to win, but normally not gaffed. The player usually has the misconception that he or she is throwing into the neck of a standard milk can, while in fact the opening is smaller.

Some law agencies report they have found cans that had openings smaller than the diameter of the game ball, but this appears to be rare.

Chapter 24

Lucky Strike Board

The attraction of Lucky Strike Board is that you get several chances to win for a dollar, and the prizes offered are large. The skill involved in winning seems minimal: toss a dime or token onto a slick board the size of a small dance floor, and hope that it lands entirely within one of the many red spots on the board. Even the name Lucky Strike conjures up the feeling that the game is easy to win.

Players stand four to five feet from the board to make their tosses. In the Lucky Strike game, rectangular decals approximately 3 inches long by 2½ inches wide are applied to the board. At the center of each rectangle is a replica of the Lucky Strike cigarette logo, about ⅞-inch in diameter.

Other games such as Circle Dime Throw and Spot Pitch use decals of stars and other shapes.

To win, the player must put a coin or round token entirely within the spot. Agents sometimes offer a booby prize such as a feather to players who get a coin partially inside the circle.

The size of the game varies from 63 rectangles to 90 rectangles per 4-foot by 7-foot section of board.

The Secret

Carnies and carnival experts agree that Lucky Strike and Spot Pitch are primarily games of chance, so the question becomes: What are the player's odds of winning?

Observation of one Spot Pitch game in the summer of 1987 led to

Players skilled in pitching coins will have an edge at a Lucky Strike Board, but winning for the average player is largely a matter of chance.

For practice, copy off these decals and glue them on cardboard at a distance of about one foot from the center of one bull's-eye to the next.

The smaller bull's-eye is for dimes, and the larger is for nickels or quarters. Try pitching coins from a distance of about four feet.

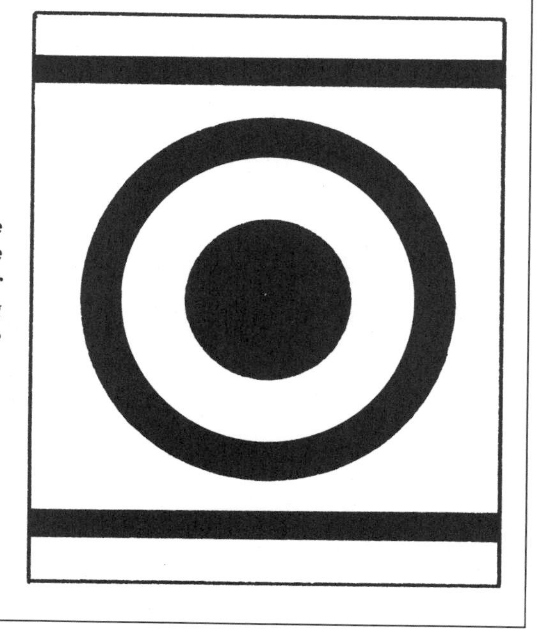

the conclusion that a person's chances of winning are good for a small prize, slim for a medium-sized prize, and very low for a choice prize.

Out of 1,318 tosses, the players won 55 small prizes consisting of foam-rubber dice that Acme Premium Supply wholesaled that year for $2 per dozen. The operator also awarded three 7-inch-tall stuffed animals that wholesaled for about $10 a dozen, and one choice stuffed animal that wholesaled for $30 to $40.

The carny operating the game confirmed that the odds calculated by the author were close to his experience. The carny figured he usually handed out a large prize for every $150 taken in.

In the game studied, dimes were tossed from a distance of about four feet onto a board area totaling 48 square feet. There were 149 targets, ranging in size from 1-inch-diameter dots to 2¾-inch-diameter circles.

The carny also said the best technique for tosses in Circle Dime Throw is the same one used in Plate Pitch: essentially, trying to make the coin land flat on the board.

FBI investigator Holmes says the FBI laboratory in Washington, D.C., conducted a 1982 study of two Spot Pitch games, collecting information from a carnival and analyzing the data in Washington. The study showed that the red circles are decals applied to a large plywood sheet entirely covered by lacquer to protect the board. Consequently, the spots are raised slightly above the playing surface.

Some law enforcement officials say the fact that the circle is raised and the board highly waxed makes this game impossible to win. Holmes says the fact that the spots are raised slightly from the playing surface "is not decisive" in whether a player will win.

However, he pointed out that a number of variables – slickness of board, raised circles, distance of throw, whether hanging prizes prevent winning throws – combine to take away the element of skill in winning.

Based strictly on the surface area of the spots for a 63-rectangle board, the FBI laboratory calculated that the normal success rate would be one win in every 107 tries, Holmes says. He says the area of the spots represents slightly less than 1 percent of the total area of the board.

But he concedes that a better technique for judging a player's odds would be through trial and error, which the FBI has not done.

Chapter 25

Ring Toss

The games of Hoop La and Ring Toss have been on the midways at least since the early 1900s, and are about as traditional on the carnival midway as cotton candy and the Ferris wheel.

They refer to a whole family of carnival games in which the object is to throw a hoop or ring and encircle the prize itself or a stand holding the prize. The rules are simple, as are the skills needed to play the games.

The chances of winning run from a sure thing to impossible, depending on how the operators set up the games.

Pitch Till You Win

This is one of the most common of all carnival games, and it appeals to parents with small children, and others who desire assured winning. In a way, Pitch Till You Win is simply a form of merchandising in which the operator essentially is "selling" a prize worth only pennies for the $1 it costs to play.

The operator gives the player a handful of wooden or plastic hoops, and the object of the game is to throw the hoop around a wooden block that has a prize affixed to it with a rubber band. Games are played with hoops that can range in size from 4 to 7 inches, inside diameter. Wooden embroidery hoops sometimes are used.

The prizes rest on two types of blocks that are equal in number. Long, five-sided blocks called "bear blocks" hold the choice prizes, and smaller, square-shaped blocks hold cheap prizes. Some bear

Hoop La, in various forms, has been on the midway since the turn of the century.

blocks have only a 1/8-inch clearance, compared to the 1-inch or more clearance of the square blocks.

As the name implies, players can keep throwing the rings until they win prizes.

It usually is extremely difficult to win the prizes attached to the long blocks because of the shape of the blocks, the angle at which players are throwing and the obstruction of the prizes themselves.

At a fair held in summer 1986 in a Detroit suburb, a carny conceded that he had never seen anyone win a choice prize, and said it would be a matter of stupendous luck if a player did. The carny demonstrated that the hoop fit over the wide wooden block, but only if dropped from the back, with the assistance of a slight push.

A perpendicular look at the face of the larger block shows that it has five sides and is longer than the diameter of the ring. One end of the block is square, and the other end tapers down to a point.

The face slants at an angle that drops toward the player. That configuration means a ring dropped directly from above the block will fit. But from where players stand, they cannot throw in an arc high enough to allow the ring to drop plumb on the block. This may occur on a rebound, but rebounds are illegal.

Since the rings cannot encircle the longer blocks, some rings inevitably will drop over the square wooden blocks with cheap prizes, ending the game.

So Pitch Till You Win is a game in which every player is assured of winning a prize, even tykes visiting the midway with their parents. But it is foolhardy to think a player can come away from the game with one of the choice prizes.

Toy Hoop La, Center Pole Pitch, Corner Pole Pitch, Cone or Pyramid Pitch

Toy Hoop La gives the player an opportunity to win a large prize, and the game requires athletic skill. However, players should examine the equipment to be sure the hoop has adequate clearance over the block holding the animal.

Acme Premium Supply Corp. sells equipment for a Hoop La game that uses a wooden block 18 inches square and about 6 inches in height. There is a lip that extends about a half inch around the top of the block to keep the legs of stuffed animals from interfering with a hoop as it circles the block.

A 1/2-inch iron pipe about 24 inches long extends vertically from one side of the block and is held in place by a pipe flange. There is a cap on top of the pipe.

Alibi agents sometimes use sleight of hand to make winning look easy with Soup Blocks.

Watch La blocks are practically impossible to hoop, so operators often put expensive watches on them as prizes.

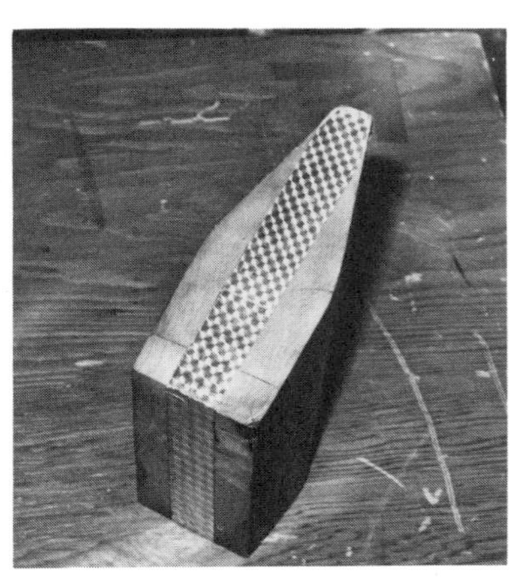

The unique shape of a Bear Block gives the illusion that it can be circled easily with a hoop tossed from the front of the joint.

The company suggests that the entire block should be placed on a support 18 to 20 inches from the ground. The company sells 25¾-inch inside diameter plastic hoops for the game, providing a clearance over the block of more than a quarter inch. Throws should be made from about five feet.

A large stuffed animal is affixed to the pipe. A player wins the prize if he or she successfully tosses the hoop so it falls completely over the block and lies flat on the ground.

Carnival equipment supplier Dawson termed a game constructed like this as "very, very fair," if the operator does not lower prizes hanging from rafters so much that winning tosses cannot be made or does not attach to the pole too-large stuffed animals that prevent the hoop from clearing the block.

The best technique to use in winning Toy Hoop La is to spin the hoop as it is being tossed and throw it so it lands as close to horizontal as possible, Dawson says.

There are variations of the basic Toy Hoop La.

In Center Pole Pitch, the prizes are attached to sticks located in the exact centers of the blocks. In Cone or Pyramid Pitch, a cone or pyramid is used instead of a stick on the block.

In Corner Pole Pitch, the stick is located near the corner of the block. Hoops usually end up encircling the corner of the block.

Carnival investigator Riedthaler says some hoops will fit over the blocks, but that is sometimes prevented by the way the prizes are attached to the sticks. In other cases, the hoops may be too small to fit over the blocks.

As in Pitch Till You Win, it is impossible to throw a hoop with some vertical motion and have it drop straight down upon a square without the benefit of a rebound.

However, some new Center Pole games allow the players to lean into the joint and hold the hoop directly over the square before dropping it. The clearance is small, but it is there.

One agent who was operating this type of game said the only way the game can be won is to "have the bounce work for you" – that is, to drop the ring so one side catches on one or two sides of the block, forcing the other side of the ring to drop over the block.

It takes practice, but it can be done, the agent said.

Watch La

The game of Watch La is played much like Pitch Till You Win, except that all the prizes are expensive watches. The player gets only a set number of rings to throw, and all the blocks are of the long variety described earlier under Pitch Till You Win.

Sometimes the blocks are tapered at the bottom to give the appearance that a ring can fit easily over the block. A carny demonstrates by dropping a ring straight down on the block, then moving the ring around at the bottom to show a relatively large amount of clearance.

In short, Watch La cannot be won.

Push Blocks or Soup Blocks

Push Blocks are square instead of wedge shaped like those used in Watch La, with faces that slant toward the players. The typical game has blocks that are about 2¾ inches square and rings about 4¼ inches in diameter.

In one game, players must slide the ring up the face of the block using only their fingertips, and encircle the block without going over the foul line at its top edge.

A carny can cheat players by holding his thumb and finger midway up the back edges of the block. When the ring makes it over the top edge of the block, it is stopped by the carny's thumb and finger – and the other side of the ring slips over the lower side of the face.

But when it's time to play for money or prizes, the carny does not hold the block. Consequently, a ring that makes it over the top edge of the block is not stopped by the fingers, and it travels too far down the back of the block. The ring then either falls off the block or is caught half-way down the block's face.

If a player does successfully encircle the block, the carny says the player's fingers were touching the ring when it went over the foul line, so the win doesn't count.

Riedthaler says carnies also use sleight of hand to make it appear that they are able to push the ring on from the front of the block, when in actuality it is placed on from the back.

Chapter 26

Fool the Guesser

There isn't anybody who secretly doesn't want to be talked about or noticed in some way. And that is the essential reason why people play Fool the Guesser.

The operator, usually calling loudly to the crowd with a bullhorn, offers for $1 to guess a person's weight, usually within three pounds for men and five pounds for women. The Age-and-Scale operator looks over the subject, writes the prediction on a pad of writing paper, then has the player step on a nearby scale. When the true answer is given, it's compared to that on the pad.

If the carny fails, the player is rewarded with the smallest prize on the shelf – or the player has the option to pay another $1 for a guess on age or month of birth, thereby getting a shot at a larger prize. Usually, the operator must get an age within two years for men and women and within a year for children. In the case of a birthday, the carny must guess within two months.

The play can continue for larger prizes, with some operators offering to take a guess on exact birthdays, or even a person's first name.

The Secret

This game is not rigged, according to law enforcement agencies. First and foremost, the prizes are of much less value than it costs to play. The operator, even if he "loses," always wins by essentially selling items worth pennies for $1. When the player decides to go for a larger prize, he or she must continue to pay.

One of the most entertaining and honest games on the midway is Fool the Guesser.

Secondly, some carnies genuinely become proficient at judging weights and ages. Good operators use plenty of theatrics before they venture their guesses, often joking with the players to keep them in good humor.

The carnies will act as if they are looking over the player, feeling the arms or shoulders of men players as if to determine solidness before writing down a prediction. Guessers usually don't touch the women players. A common rule of thumb is that predictions on weight and age are low rather than high, so the player is flattered even though the operator misses.

In predicting the month of birth within two months, the chance is 1 in 4 that the operator will guess correctly. Those odds can be enhanced if the Guesser is observant and the player is wearing a birthstone.

When they are called upon to guess the first name of a person, Guessers usually ask for the first initial. Then they ask whether the name is the legal name or a nickname. If it is a nickname, the operator asks for the first letter of the legal name.

Operators who travel the same circuit each year can become familiar with the ethnic heritage of a city, and from that deduce the most likely first names of the people raised there. Some Guessers also "tune" their ears so they can guess the general birthplace of a person by his or her accent.

Fool the Guesser is good, clean fun that requires no skill on the part of the player. With carnies who are seasoned and quick-witted, it can be a game that is as much fun for the crowd as it is for the contestant. Where else these days can someone get that much entertainment for $1 – and a possible souvenir of the carnival to boot?

Chapter 27

Tip 'Em Over

The equipment used in making a Tip 'Em Over is familiar to everyone: two empty Coca Cola bottles, a softball or baseball and a polished playing board. The object of the game is simply to roll or throw the ball and knock down two bottles standing side by side.

There are two versions of the game, one played on a counter top at chest level and one played at ground level. The ground-level version, the older of the two games, is losing popularity on the midway. Carnival equipment supplier Dawson says he doesn't expect to see the ground-level version on any midways in the 1990s.

The Secret

The counter-top version of Tip 'Em Over, also called Coke Roll, can be won by striking the two bottles simultaneously in their centers with the ball. That sounds easy enough, but the apparent simplicity of the game is deceiving.

The "regulation" softball agents offer to players is really a lightweight, hard-foam ball the size of a softball and covered with a softball's leather skin. The lightweight ball can be given enough energy to knock over the two 6½-fluid-ounce bottles of Coke, but the shot must hit the faces of the bottles dead on.

In an article he wrote in 1984, Donald Patterson, captain with the Cheyenne, Wyo., Police Department, calculated that the odds against the player winning Coke Roll Game are 1 in 35, depending on the weight of the ball used, the skill of the player and the slickness of the

In the countertop version of Tip 'Em Over, players have to knock down both bottles with an ultralight softball.

playing board.

Carnival consultant Snyder says the game is difficult because it is often operated from chest height, so a player cannot roll the ball with as much force or accuracy as in bowling. He also says a softball does not roll perfectly straight because of its stitches.

The ground-level version of Tip 'Em Over is primarily a game of skill, Dawson says. The bottles usually are placed side by side, with a space of about ¼-inch between them. The small space between the bottles prevents a player from knocking over one bottle that consequently bowls over the other bottle.

Dawson's company, Acme Premium Supply Corp., suggests that the game be played with a softball-sized ball of cork that has been wrapped with plastic tape.

The bottles rest on an 8-by-12-inch Masonite-covered board on the ground, and throws are made from about five feet. All throws are made underhand, and the player needs only to knock over the bottles once.

Dawson says the best way to win is to simultaneously strike the necks of the two bottles squarely without hitting the board. Literature from Acme Premium suggests that the operator should not use prizes that cost more than twice the amount per play.

"Normally, a player will win about one out of five times, but some players will become quite good," the literature states. "Be sure to have a sign posted, limiting the number of prizes a player can win."

Dawson says he doesn't expect to see the ground-level version of Tip 'Em Over Coke on the midway of the 1990 carnival season. "It is a very old, old game and there are very, very few of them left."

He says the counter-top version is "a good game, but it depends on the agent. Some work the game strong."

Words of Caution

Even though their odds are enhanced greatly by using a hard-foam softball, some agents decide to gaff the countertop version of Coke Roll by the way they set up the bottles. If one of the bottles is set slightly closer to the player, it may be impossible to win, Patterson says in the article he wrote for the Federal Bureau of Investigation.

The reason is that a ball rolled straight forward expends all of its energy knocking over the foremost bottle, and the second bottle simply slides on the nearly frictionless surface.

James Story, detective with the Oklahoma City Police Department, says his agency arrested four carnival agents during the 1986 state fair in Oklahoma City for cheating people by offsetting the coke bottles. Story says three of the four pleaded guilty to taking money under false pretenses, and the fourth was convicted on the same charge.

To protect players and prevent agents from making an honest mistake, the Oklahoma City Police Department requires that a black line be drawn across the back of the playing field where bottles are set. That way, both player and agent can see whether the bottles are even, Story says.

Carnival investigator Riedthaler says operators of the Coke Roll Game require a player to roll the ball twice for a large prize so they can detect which hand the player favors. Operators then set the bottles up accordingly: for a right-handed player, the second bottle is set to the left of the bottle in the forefront; the opposite is done for someone who is left-handed.

It is possible to knock over bottles that are offset if the player rolls the ball from an angle, but this may be a foul under some agents' rules. Those who decide to try their hands at Coke Roll ought to ask the operator about all the conditions under which a play is called foul.

Some carnies declare that the players lose when the bottles hit the sides of the board before falling, while others use the alibi that the player's hand went past the foul line during the roll.

In summary, the counter-top version of Tip 'Em Over has a reputation in police circles for being a game that can easily be gaffed. Before players hand over their dollars, they should handle the game ball to determine its weight, observe whether operators set the bottles flush with the players, and find out specifically when fouls are called.

How to Build Your Own Game

The odds of winning Tip 'Em Over on the midway can be improved with practice, if the game is played legitimately. It is a rather simple game to build at home, consisting of a playing board with a slick surface, two 6½-ounce Coke bottles and a cheap softball.

Materials and tools needed to construct a Coke Roll Game: a sheet of ½-inch plywood 22¼ inches by 47 inches, sandpaper, 1-pint can of high-gloss polyurethane or shellac, red paint, brush, two pieces of ¾-inch pine board 3½ inches by 39½ inches, one piece ¾-inch pine board 3½ inches by 22¼ inches, and some small nails.

Sand the finish side of the plywood sheet with coarse, medium, and then fine sandpaper to get a smooth surface. Paint a ½-inch-wide red foul line 8 inches from one end of the board. Use masking tape to obtain a straight edge on the line.

Apply the high-gloss polyurethane or shellac to the sanded side of the board, let dry, buff with 150-grit or fine sandpaper to remove bumps, and wipe clean. Apply more coats in this manner until the surface is slick.

For a finished appearance, paint the pine board sides of the game any color of your choosing. With nails, attach the smaller board opposite the foul line and the longer two pieces as sides.

It may be difficult to obtain two 6½-fluid-ounce Coke bottles, but any small soda bottles will do. Coke bottles are preferable because their weight and distinctive shape make them more of a challenge to knock down. Check with party stores or soft-drink distributors to see whether they carry the smaller sizes. If not, check with antique bottle collectors.

If you find it is too easy to knock over the bottles with a regulation-weight softball, lighten the ball by tearing off the cover, hollowing out much of the cork core, and stitching the cover back on. You will be surprised how much more difficult it is to knock over the bottles with a ball that is only two or three ounces lighter.

Chapter 28

Ladder Climb

The Ladder Climb is one of those midway games that is almost as much fun to watch as it is to play. The object of the game is to crawl up a rope ladder consisting of nine rungs and ring a bell at the top.

It looks easy enough as the carnies scramble up and down with the dexterity of monkeys. But when adventuresome players try to imitate the carnies, they spin and fall onto a large pillow or bed of straw – rarely getting past the third rung.

What makes the game a challenge and entertaining is that both ends of the ladder pivot on swivels. This is strictly a game of skill, dependent upon the player's balance. Agents practice for hours before they can climb the rope ladder with the ease they display.

Ladder Climb – formerly known by the name Indian Rope Trick – has been around for years, according to June Hardin, president of Wapello Fabrications Inc. Carnival operators used to make the rope ladder and buy inflatable safety mats from Wapello Fabrications before the company began manufacturing a complete version of the game, Hardin says.

A typical Ladder Climb has rungs about 2 feet long that are separated by about 16½ inches, so there is plenty of room for a player to climb.

The prizes being awarded are among the largest on the midway – and that should be a tipoff on the amount of skill necessary to win.

(Clockwise from top left): The carn steadies his ascent with his left foo as he steps on the first rung. He al ways places his hands on the ropes not on the rungs. The carny balance with his left hand and right foot, be fore moving his right hand and lef foot to the next rung.

(Clockwise from top left): He keeps his knees to the outside to prevent catching his foot on a lower rung while ascending the ladder. The carny keeps his body low and in the center of the ladder during the ascent. He rings the bell.

The Secret

Hardin says climbing the rope ladder is a test of balance. The No. 1 rule in climbing is that the player counterbalances one action with another: When you extend your right hand, move your left leg at the same time onto the next rung, then procede with left hand, right leg, etc. A player can get an idea of this motion by scooting that way across the floor.

Another tip is to steady yourself with your leg between the ropes when you are starting (see first photo in series). Most carnies hold on to the rope between the rungs, and do not grasp the rungs themselves.

It also is best to extend and point the toes when moving your foot to the next rung, so it doesn't catch on the bottom of a rung and cause a spill.

Because Ladder Climb is primarily a test of skill, with large prizes awarded to winners, it is usually a more expensive game to play. At one fair where other games were charging $1 per try, the Ladder Climb was charging $1.50. Some Ladder Climbs also have a rule that a player is allowed to win only one prize a day.

Chapter 29

Whiffle Ball Flukey Ball

Playing the Whiffle Ball game is a lot like trying free throws in basketball: It looks easy until you step up to the line and shoot. Whiffle Ball and basketball have some similarities, the most prominent being that the object of the game is to get a ball into a basket.

But as its name suggests, the player must bounce a Whiffle ball or similar lightweight ball off a backboard and have it fall into the basket to win. The game usually offers decent prizes, and players can better their chances at winning through practice.

Whiffle Ball has an unsavory cousin that goes under various names, including Flukey, Fluken or Flukum Ball. Flukey cheats players through the use of a gaffed Whiffle ball that makes it almost impossible to complete a fair shot. Fortunately, Flukum Ball is becoming more scarce on the midways.

The only equipment that seems to be common to all Whiffle Ball games is the use of a lightweight ball and a board that rests at an angle. Probably more than any other carnival game, Whiffle Ball games have no consistency in width or height. Vastly different sizes and shapes can even be found on the same midway at larger fairs.

In some games, players lean their thighs against a rail and get as close as possible to the board when they shoot. In other games, players place their toes up against a board on the ground and try to stretch close to the Whiffle Ball board. However, skill in winning one game can extend to winning a different version.

Without any practice, Whiffle Ball is a difficult game to win. In a

Whiffle Ball has become a very popular game on the midway in the past few years.

two-hour observation at a state fair, the author saw only six people get a ball in the basket out of a total of 933 attempts by all people playing during that time.

The boards were six feet from the players, and the carnies were using king-sized Whiffle balls. The boards, 4 feet long and 18 inches wide, were at an angle of about 25 degrees from vertical.

What drew the crowds was the prize: medium-sized Spuds MacKenzie stuffed dogs that probably wholesale for $6 to $8 apiece. Players paid $1 per throw, although some of the carnies offered three balls for $2.

The Secret

T.J., a second-generation carny who specializes in Whiffle Ball, says there are several methods of winning the game. Old-time carnies, many of whom once worked Flukey games, stand straight up and throw the ball in an arc higher than their heads. The ball barely touches the bottom edge of the board as it falls from the arc. But T.J. revealed easier techniques of finding the "sweet spot" – the ideal spot to bounce the ball.

First, he says, never toss the ball so it makes a direct hit low against the board. The ball will only rebound back to you. Rebound off the top of the board and try to skim the ball off the surface, rather than toss a direct hit.

Although tall people with a long reach have an advantage in this game, a short person can win handily if he or she throws the ball right. If it is a game that encourages leaning, the player should lean in as far as possible and start the throw with the ball low – even touching the ball to the ground first.

From then on, however, the techniques differ among carnies. Some will raise their arms up as high and close to the board as they can, and let the ball roll off their fingertips so that it just skims the board on its way down.

Others raise their arms high and close to the board and give a slight toss so that the ball skims the board on its way up, and then arcs back down into the basket.

Words of Caution

Ask the carny to demonstrate how the game is played. In a fair game, the carny will stand where the players stand, and make the shot using the same ball that will be given to players. If a carny can't do that for you, chances are you won't be able to do it either.

If a carny struggles but makes a shot after several tries, it may be that the board is set at too tough an angle for a successful shot by the

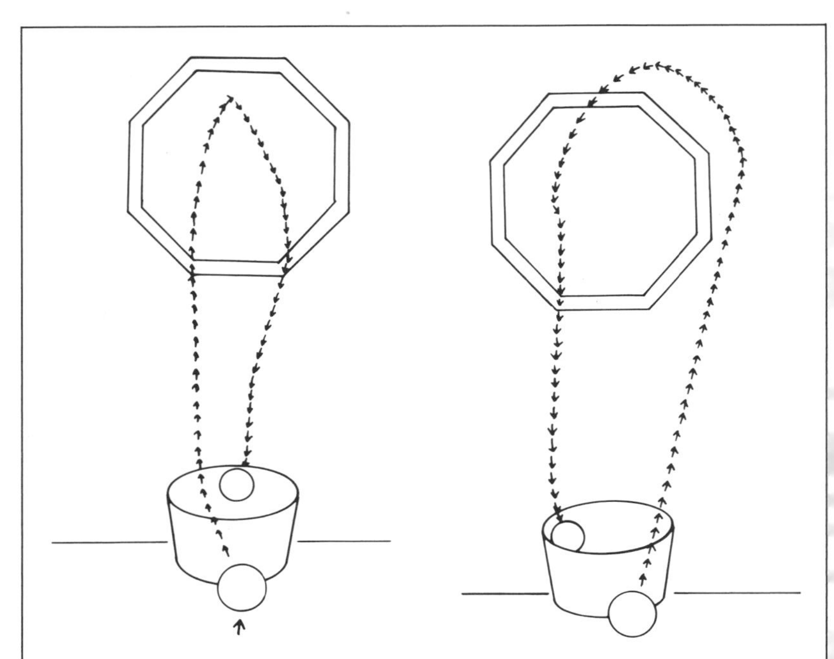

Some carnies prefer to toss the ball so it just nicks the top of the board on its ascent (left). Other carnies toss the ball slightly higher than the board, letting it rebound on its descent.

average person. In that case, it may be best to look for an easier game.

Law enforcement agencies surveyed for this book warned about Flukey Ball and cited a couple of simple ways to detect this gaffed game. Watch what kind of ball is used by the carny to demonstrate how to win, and note whether the ball is taped. Carnies sometimes use solid trash baskets in Flukey Ball so players cannot see agents switching balls. Most Whiffle Ball games use perforated baskets.

In Flukey Ball, the player usually, but not always, must make two shots to win. In Whiffle Ball, the player needs to make only one shot.

Flukey Ball relies on a Whiffle ball that has been tampered with. Normal Whiffle balls tend to have too much bounce to fall into the basket. Unscrupulous operators deaden the ball's bounce by cutting a slice in the ball and concealing it with tape, or by covering the holes with tape and filling the ball with cotton, powdered graphite or talcum powder.

Using the gaffed ball, the agent demonstrates how easy it is to rebound the ball into the basket. But in retrieving the ball for a player, the agent grabs an identical-looking "live" ball that is already in the bottom of the basket.

How to Build Your Own Game

You can improve your chances of winning by practicing Whiffle Ball at home, provided your homemade game approximates what you find at the carnival. It is fairly easy to construct a Whiffle Ball game that looks like a stop sign, using hand tools, wood scraps and a little paint. And it's a fun game to have around the house for rainy-day activity.

Materials and tools needed: saw, hammer, screwdriver, straightedge, tape measure, wood screws, 3-inch utility hinge, drill, masking tape, red and white paint, paint brush, razor or X-acto knife, 19½-inch square of any thickness plywood, three 4-foot-long 2-by-4s, king-sized Wiffle ball, plastic clothes basket.

Mark points 5¾ inches from each corner on all four sides of the plywood square, and draw lines to connect adjacent points. Put masking tape on both sides of the board along the lines before sawing. This prevents the plywood from splitting and leaving jagged edges. Saw off the four triangular "ears": This will produce an octagon-shaped stop sign.

Mark three holes 2 inches from the edge of two opposite sides of the sign, and drill pilot holes the right diameter to fit wood screws. Attach two of the 2-by-4s with wood screws to make legs for the back of the sign. To ease the effort of getting the screws into the 2-by-4s, put some soap on the threads of the screws.

Paint the sign and the third 2-by-4 entirely red. If you want an attractive finish, it is best to sand the sign before painting.

When the sign is dry, cover its entire face with masking tape. Draw a ½-inch border all along the edge around the sign. Refer to the diagram to measure the letters, and draw them over the masking tape.

Cut out the letters and edging with a razor or knife, remove the excess masking tape, and paint over the cut-out areas with white paint. When the paint is dry, remove all the masking tape, and you will be impressed with the quality of your "stop sign."

Attach the hinge to the back of the sign at the top midpoint, and attach the third leg. Squeeze a plastic clothes basket between the legs, and the game is ready to play.

If you want to practice the type of game that permits leaning, you may wish to cut a 2-by-4 the width of a door. Then place the board

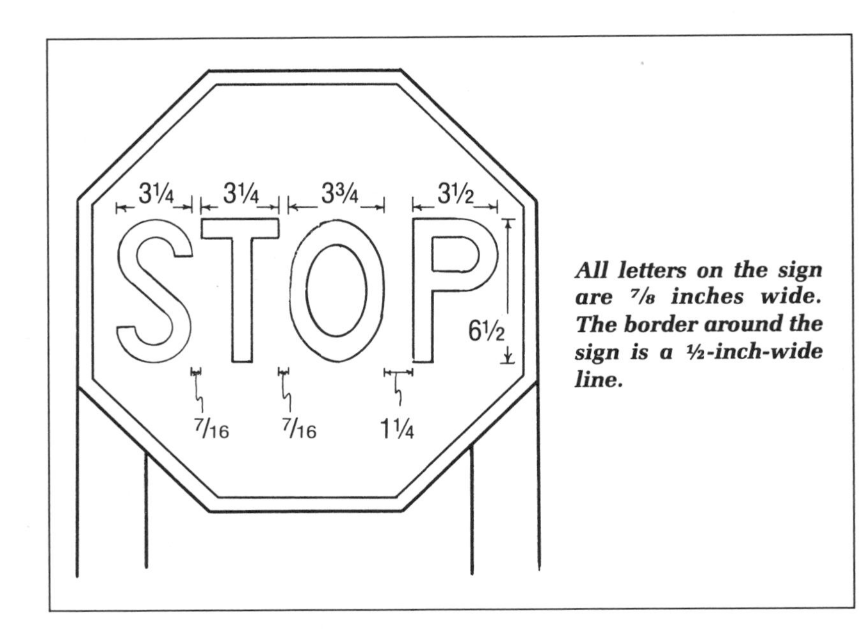

All letters on the sign are 7/8 inches wide. The border around the sign is a ½-inch-wide line.

against the doorstop at a comfortable height.

Chapter 30

High Striker

For the young man who wants to show off his muscle to his sweetheart, there probably isn't a game on the midway that can beat High Striker. It has everything for a showoff: a huge maul that looks heavy enough to split boulders, a 21-foot track that towers over the crowd, and a gong that rings loud and clear whenever someone makes a solid hit.

Jim Hatchett, owner of the J.A. Hatchett Mfg. Co. in Rolla, Mo., says High Striker has remained a popular game for decades because of its appeal to people who want to test their strength – and prove it to others.

The High Striker Hatchett manufactures has been around for at least 50 years. He bought the business in 1982 from I.T. Fuller, a Rolla native who had manufactured the game for 22 years. Fuller got the idea to build High Strikers from an old carny.

Hatchett's High Striker for adult males is 21 feet tall and uses a 7-pound to 8-pound maul. A cast-iron striker weighing a little under a half pound rests at the bottom of the tower on one end of a heavy beam that pivots. On the other end of the beam is a thick rubber cushion that is the target the player attempts to hit with the maul.

The object of the game is to hit the cushion hard enough with the maul to send the striker sliding up the 1½-inch-wide metal track far enough to ring a 12-inch gong. All along the track are numbers running to 2,300 and humorous sayings that rate a person's strength. Hit the cushion wrong and you may be labeled a "sick duck" or a

High Strikers such as this one are difficult to gaff because the weight travels along a metal track instead of a wire cable.

"deadhead." Hit it right and you can call yourself a "he-man."

For women and children, Hatchett manufactures a shorter version of High Striker that employs a 4-pound to 5-pound maul.

The Secret

The High Striker is a true test of a person's strength and skill in swinging a maul and landing a blow accurately.

"The trade secret is to hit the pad squarely, just as if you were splitting wood," Hatchett says. The trick is to try to have the face of the maul land flat against the surface of the cushion.

The cost of play and the prizes offered depend on where the carnival is operating. At one East Coast amusement park, it costs $1 a whack and no prizes are given, because the game usually is played as a contest of strength between friends. Other places allow a patron three whacks for 50 cents.

Recently, at a carnival in Michigan, an operator using one of Hatchett's games was offering three whacks for $1. If the customer rang the gong once, he received a feather. If the gong was rung twice, a small prize was awarded. If the gong sounded three times, the prize was a 6-inch-long plush toy.

Hatchett says he has seen early-day models that were gaffed so the agent quickly and easily could make it impossible for someone to ring the bell. These High Strikers used several guy wires that held up the tower. Unknown to the players, one of the guy wires led from a stake directly down the front of the tower. The striker traveled along this wire.

The unscrupulous agent would lean up against the phony guy wire and keep it taut enough so the mark could ring the bell on the first and second tries. But when it came time for the player to take the third swing, the agent would stop leaning on the wire. With the wire slack, the striker brushed against the tower as it traveled skyward, and friction prevented it from reaching the gong. The player had no chance to ring the gong and win the grand prize for three rings.

Hatchett says the game he manufactures can be adjusted so it takes a harder swing to ring the gong, but he says the game is the same for everybody, once it is set. Hatchett advises carnies who buy his game that they should never adjust it so tight that the bell cannot be rung. The sound of the gong is like advertising, and it never fails to draw a tip, he says.

Chapter 31

Five Pin

For those who fancy themselves bowlers, these games look so easy to win that it seems almost unfair to the carnies. Rather than try to knock down the 10 pins in a regulation bowling game, players in this tabletop version of bowling are asked to knock over only five pins in two tries, or two or three pins in one try. And the prizes awarded usually are some of the largest on the midway.

But this pint-sized bowling game is deceptively hard to beat – so much so that it is strictly a matter of luck if you win, law enforcement agents say.

It also is a game that is very easy to gaff so it cannot be won, they say.

The game can be played with two, three or five wooden pins and a hard rubber or wooden ball. The object of the game is to roll the ball down an alley four feet long and knock down all the pins. The player gets one ball in Two Pin or Three Pin, and two balls in Five Pin.

In Three Pin, the agent sets the bases of the pins so they are touching each other in a line, and then pulls the middle pin back. In Five Pin, the agent pulls the second and fourth pins back. In Two Pin, the places for the pins are marked by two circles drawn on the alley.

The Secret

One carny who operated a Five Pin game says the only way to win is for the player to aim straight at the second pin in Three Pin and the second and fourth pins in Five Pin. The ball will catch the sides of

Players have to be cautious of Five Pin because the pins can be set so it is impossible to knock them all over in two tries.

the front pins and bowl over the back pin, he says.

However, the game can be easily set up so the player cannot win even with a perfectly placed shot. That is because the front pins can be placed at a distance from each other that equals the diameter of the ball. Under such a setup, the ball is able to take out only two of the three pins – one front pin and the back pin.

In the Two Pin game, the carny places the pins within two circles that are larger than the bases of the pins. An agent who wants to run the game legitimately puts the bases of the pins inside the circles and as close together as possible. To gaff the game, the carny puts the pins inside the circles, but as far away from each other as possible, carnival investigator Riedthaler says.

Agents sometimes give carnivalgoers a free shot to encourage play, and the player often wins in practice. Why? Because for the practice shot, the agent sets the pins closer together than the diameter of the ball.

Agents also use a crude sleight of hand when they demonstrate how the game can be won. From inside the joint, the agent will roll the ball toward the pins and then brush the pins with his arm to knock them down. The player can plainly see that the agent, not the ball, knocked the pins down, but the ruse gives the impression that the game is easy to win.

What makes the pin games deceptive is the short distance the balls are rolled, the relatively wide bases of the pins, and the light weight of the pins.

How to Make Your Own Game

This is not the sort of game in which the player improves his chances of winning with practice. The game relies too heavily on whether the agent is playing fair – something that is difficult for the player to judge at the midway.

However, if you are interested in making your own tabletop version of the game to entertain your friends, here are the general dimensions for a regular Three Pin or Five Pin game you might find at the carnival.

With a 3¼-inch-diameter ball, the wooden pins are 4¼ inches tall with 1¾-inch-diameter bases. The vertical part of the pin is half-inch doweling leading down to a conelike base about ⅞-inch high.

The ball most carnies use is taken from a Skee-Ball game, which isn't readily available to the public. Balls from a boccie or croquet set or other game may be used if the height and width of the pins are altered accordingly. To find the correct diameter for the base of each pin, take the diameter of the ball, add a quarter-inch, then divide by

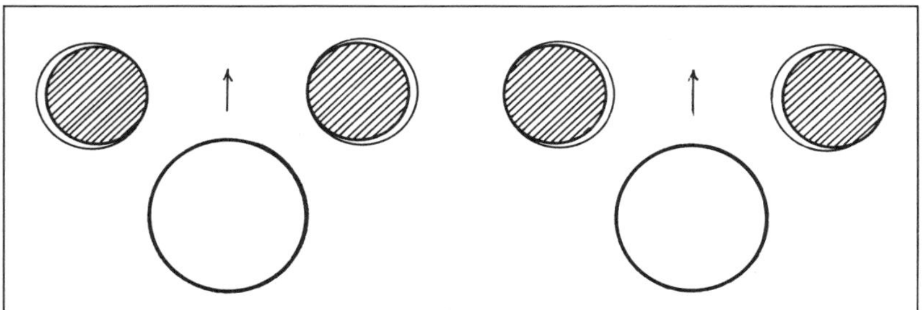

If the pins are set on the closest points between the two circles, the game can be won (left). If the pins are set on the farthest points of the two circles, the ball can roll through without touching either pin.

two. The height of the pin should be about an inch more than the diameter of the ball.

The playing board is made up of two pieces of ½-inch plywood: one 4 feet by 2 feet, and one 45 inches by 18 inches. The smaller piece of plywood is glued to the larger piece flush at one end, with the center lines of the two pieces of board lying over each other. This creates two alleyways in which the agent returns the ball to the players, and one at the back that stops the ball. A foul line can be painted on the top piece of plywood 1 foot in from the flush end.

When it is completed, the entire board can be covered with a high-gloss polyurethane or shellac.

Build the sides and back of the game with three pieces of ¾-inch by 3½-inch pine board. If the boards are to be simply nailed into the plywood, the sides are 36 inches long and the back is 25½ inches long.

Chapter 32

String Pull

The present-day version of String Pull is much the same as the game played 70 years ago under the name Post Office String Game.

The game consists of perhaps 100 ⅛-inch-diameter ropes attached to prizes or paper tags that signify prizes. The strings run from the prizes or tags arranged on back shelves, over a rafter of the joint, through a hoop and into the operator's hand. Sometimes, operators hold a collar containing the ends of the strings, rather than the strings themselves.

As the name suggests, the player pays to pull one of the strings to find which prize he or she has won. String Pull, therefore, is a game of chance.

The player may consider playing a String Pull that is operated as a hanky pank, meaning that every player is awarded some prize. In this case, it is highly unlikely that the player will win the choice prizes, and the player should be prepared to walk away with only a piece of slum.

The game should not be played if a player can lose – that is, if some strings offer no prizes. It should never be played if the agent offers to give a player a cash bonus, return the cost of playing and award a large prize if he or she pulls a lucky string – because that means the game is surely gaffed.

The Secret

String Pull has a reputation among law enforcement agents and

String Pull can be an entertaining game, but don't count on winning large prizes. (Photo courtesy of William Riedthaler)

carnival experts for being gaffed. There are several ways in which the game can be operated so players have no chance of winning the choice prizes that lured them in the first place.

A.K. Brill, in his construction plans for carnival games, advises operators to "have real costly prizes for bait." A string to a choice prize should be folded back in the agent's hand and obscured by the other strings, so the player "does not get a chance to pull it," Brill writes.

In this way, the operator can make players think that the game is legitimate because, when he yanks on the bunch of strings, all the prizes rise.

An operator should have the choice-prize string folded back so it "can be released if necessary" and no gaff can be detected by suspicious players, Brill writes. Otherwise, "some well-heeled player might buy all the strings, and if the big prize doesn't come up, you will have a riot."

Carnival investigator Riedthaler reports that in some games he has examined, the strings from choice prizes never run past the rafter into the hoop.

Former carny Sorrows writes that some unscrupulous carnies attach the strings of desirable prizes to a pedal hidden under the counter. When the operator yanks on the bunch of strings, he or she also steps on the secret pedal, causing the choice prizes to rise and giving the illusion that the game is honest.

Chapter 33

Bottle Stand

Bottle Stand is a deceptively simple game in which players use their fingers or a notched stick of wood to right a beer or Coke bottle lying at about a 45-degree angle.

In theory, the bottle can be righted if the player exerts a slow and steady pressure on the bottle neck.

In practice, it is a rigged game that players should avoid. There are gaffs involved that make this game a bad bet to play on the midway.

It is difficult to give an exact physical description of Bottle Stand, also known as Push-Up Coke, because the game is homemade.

In one game, the bottle is placed on a cloth-covered board about a foot square. The board has adjustment screws on two corners so it can be given a downward slope away from the player. The neck of the bottle is held at an angle by a two-tined carving fork, and players use their fingers or a notched wooden stick to right the bottle.

Another game uses a cloth-covered block about 4 inches thick and slightly wider than the diameter of the bottle's bottom. The neck of the bottle is held up by a 10-inch length of wooden ruler that has a "V" notch cut on its end, and the player uses a carving fork to right the bottle.

The Secret

In directions on building a Push-Up Coke game, A.K. Brill writes that operators sometimes place a matchstick under the cloth less than halfway from the front edge of the block or board so the bottle will always topple after it reaches a vertical position.

Bottle Stand relies on the way weight is distributed in a bottle and whether theboard is level. (Photo courtesy of William Riedthaler)

Carnival investigator Riedthaler reports that carnies also gaff the game by insuring that the weight of the bottle is distributed so the bottle will fall backward as it reaches vertical.

The weight of almost every bottle is unevenly distributed when it is manufactured. Carnies find the heavier side of the bottle by corking the mouth and floating it in a tub of water. The heavier part of the bottle naturally floats downward in the water.

To gaff the game so the player will lose, the carny places the bottle with the heavier side skyward. As the player lifts the bottle nearer the vertical position, its extra weight pulls the bottle down the incline swiftly and causes it to topple.

If the lighter half is skyward, the bottle can be righted.

Former carny Sorrows writes that operators also gaff the game by changing the level of the board so it has a steeper incline. They do this by resting the two front screws of the board on holes in the counter that are covered by cloth. When they want to make the incline steeper, they simply move the board so the screws no longer rest in the holes.

Or the operators may rest the back edge of the board on a thin strip of wood on the counter that is hidden by the cloth. To increase the incline, they move the board off the strip of wood.

Chapter 34

Razzle Dazzle

Like the devil, Razzle Dazzle appears in various forms and under many names. It is the most vicious game on the midway, and the author cannot understand why a carnival sponsor would allow Razzle or its cousins to operate on the premises.

Police files are loaded with reports of gullible people from all walks of life having been cheated out of thousands of dollars each, playing Razzle. Gambling expert John Scarne wrote that an American industrialist once lost $95,000 playing Razzle in Havana, Cuba, in the 1950s.

Never play this game. And advise others not to play. It is to be hoped that, as carnivalgoers become better educated and avoid Razzle scams, the flatties that operate these games will disappear from the midway.

It should be obvious that Razzle games are frauds because of the prizes awarded or the payoffs offered for wagers. Some Razzles have color TV sets, expensive stereos, watches or jewelry as prizes. Others offer to pay out $10 for every $1 spent by a player who wins.

Razzle made its appearance in the early 1940s in the United States as a variation on the gaffed form of Roll Down, Scarne said. Grifters embraced Razzle because the game can be transported easily in a suitcase and it does not have a mechanical gaff. In fact, the operator cheats in favor of the player at the beginning of the game as a way to enhance interest.

Razzle also is largely self-working because the odds against the

PLAY FOOTBALL

100 YARDS OR OVER WIN

29
BONUS
INSURED

18 H. P.	42 20 Yards	38 H P	15 15 Yards	19 H P.	41 15 Yards	37 H. P	14 15 Yards
9 100 Yards	28	48 100 Yards	26	8 100 Yards	30	47 100 Yards	27
32	44 50 Yards	25	13 30 Yards	31	43 50 Yards	24	12 50 Yards
46 100 Yards	34	11 100 Yards	23	45 50 Yards	33	10 100 Yards	22 Add
36 Prize	16 10 Yards	21 Free	40 5 Yards	35 Free	17 5 Yards	20 Prize	39 2 Yards

Yards Good Only While Playing - - Not Transferable - - VOID After Leaving Stand

No. 29 DOES NOT WIN   BLACK NUMBERS DO NOT WIN   ALWAYS DOUBLE ON No. 29

An essential part of every Razzle Dazzle game is use of a conversion chart to determine how many points a players has won. While it appears to players that they will receive points or prizes more than half the times they play, in reality, the odds are stacked against them. (Chart courtesy of William Riedthaler)

player winning are astronomical. And there is a way that operators can make it impossible for a player to win.

Finally, Razzle provides a way for the operator to raise the stakes from a few dollars to hundreds of dollars in a matter of a few minutes.

Razzle goes under various names because it can be played with marbles, dice, darts, miniature footballs, clothespins, numbered pingpong balls, or six-, eight- or 10-sided logs called Baffle Blocks.

The object may be to reach 100 yards in Play Football, 100 runs in Play Baseball, 100 miles in Auto Races or achieve 10 points in the game Ten Points.

But one element common to all Razzle games is the use of a conversion chart. The chart tells the player how many points he or she has won.

The chart also lists Razzle's complicated but vague rules, which players only begin to understand after they start playing. One rule common to all Razzles is that several times during the game, the player is required to double or triple the amount per play, or risk immediate loss.

This doubling-up rule is the method the operator uses to fleece just one player of thousands of dollars. For instance, a $1 wager becomes a $1,024 wager in just 10 turns if the wager is doubled each turn, according to statistics provided by the laboratory division of the Federal Bureau of Investigation in Washington, D.C.

Players rarely ask in advance the meaning of certain terms on the chart such as bonus, prize, or "H.P." – which can mean anything the operator chooses, including half point, half pint of beverage, or house prize such as a cheap toy.

Finally, operators reckon the scores obtained by the player so quickly that the player cannot double-check the total. This allows the operator to cheat at will, for or against the player as the need arises.

Probably the most popular form of Razzle is Play Football, where the player rolls eight marbles onto a playing board that has 143 holes. Each of the holes bears a number from 1 through 6.

A player has the possibility of rolling 41 different scores, ranging from a low of 8 to a high of 48.

After a player spills the marbles onto the board, the operator tallies the score and refers to the conversion chart to determine how many yards the player will receive toward his or her goal. For instance, a player gets 100 yards and immediately wins the game if he or she rolls an 8, 9, 47 or 48. If the player rolls a 10 or 46, he or she receives 50 yards, etc.

But the operator now resorts to some false logic to entice the player to join in the game. The agent states that the chart gives out a total of 852 yards for the 41 scores possible, so the player should receive slightly more than 20 yards per roll on the average.

Players then think they can get 100 yards in five rolls and win a

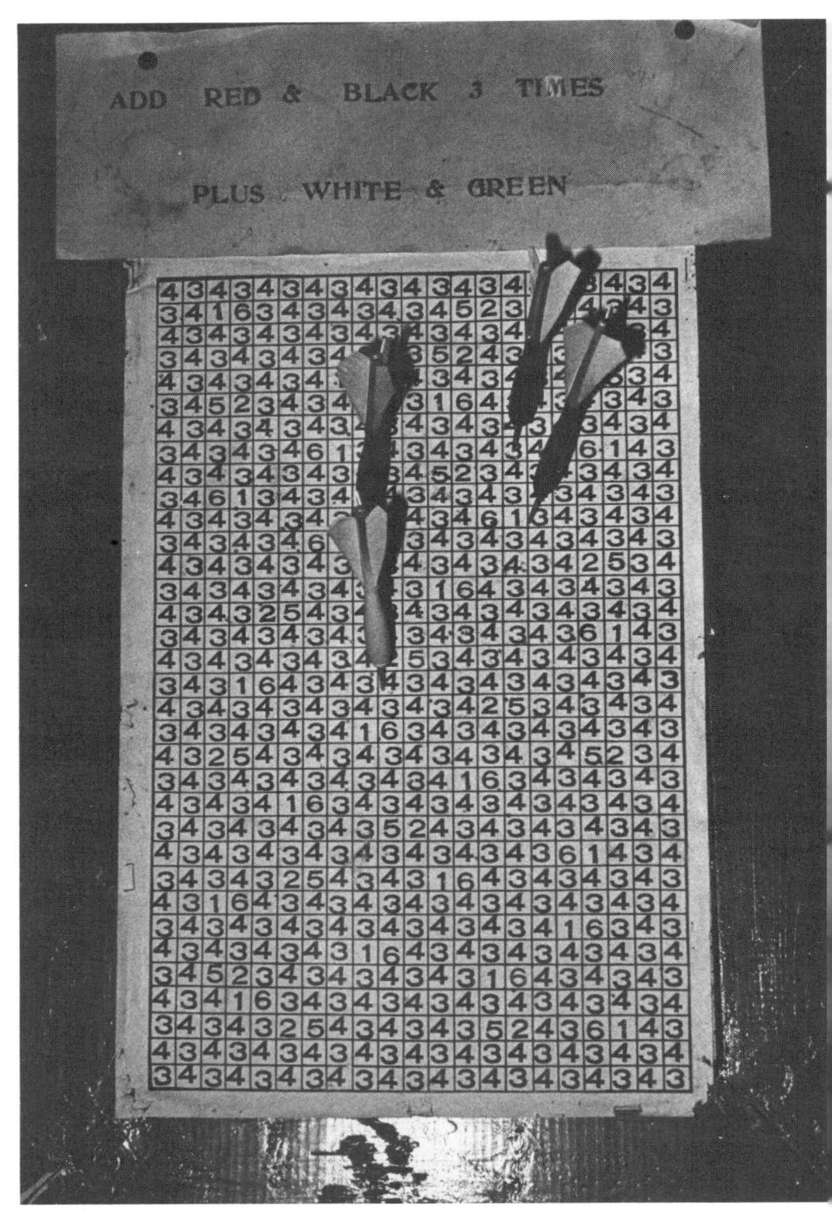

In this form of Razzle, the player tosses darts at numbers, and a score is calculated from the numbers hit and the color of the dart. The flattie then changes the score into yards or miles by using a conversion chart.

color TV set or receive a 10-to-1 payoff on their money with the risk of only $5.

What the players don't recognize is that they do not receive yards if they roll 21 of the 41 possible scores, and that these 21 combinations are the most likely to occur. This is because there are about four times as many 3s and 4s on the board as there are 1s and 6s.

The operator smoothes over that glaring flaw by explaining that the player receives something, such as a free roll or a cheap toy, in nine of the 21 combinations that don't result in yardage. So the player naturally assumes he or she receives something in rolling either the 20 combinations that result in yardage or the nine that result in some non-yardage award.

But players can actually lose yards if they roll some numbers, and they must double the amount of money per play if they roll other frequently occurring numbers, such as the number 29.

So how many rolls would it take to achieve 100 yards? Assuming that yards cannot be taken away, the player would have to roll 6,011 times to win, according to an FBI study.

There is the possibility that the player will roll an 8, 9, 47 or 48 on the first roll and win the game. However the FBI calculated that the chance of someone rolling 8 or 48 would be one in every 10.7 million rolls. The chance of someone rolling 9 or 47 would be one in every 2.2 million rolls.

A Razzle game that uses eight dice instead of marbles yields slightly better odds (see table). The odds against rolling 8 or 48 are about 840,000 to one, and the odds against rolling 9 or 47 are about 105,000 to one.

The odds indicate the incredible amount of money it would take to win at Razzle, because the bets are doubled or trebled every few rolls. Upon request of the Sacramento County district attorney's office in Sacramento, Calif., a mathematics professor in 1974 concluded that it would cost one septillion dollars (the number 1 followed by 24 zeros) for a player to win a Razzle game that used darts, assuming the player had no dart-throwing skill.

Assuming that the player possessed a great deal of skill, the professor concluded that the average cost of winning would be $4,425 at 50 cents per play.

However, operators employ a technique called the "fast count" that removes any possibility that players can win at Razzle, regardless of how remote those chances are.

In a fast count, agents scoop up the marbles, dice or darts immediately after they are thrown, call out numbers that may not be correct, and give an immediate tally that also may be wrong. Players usually

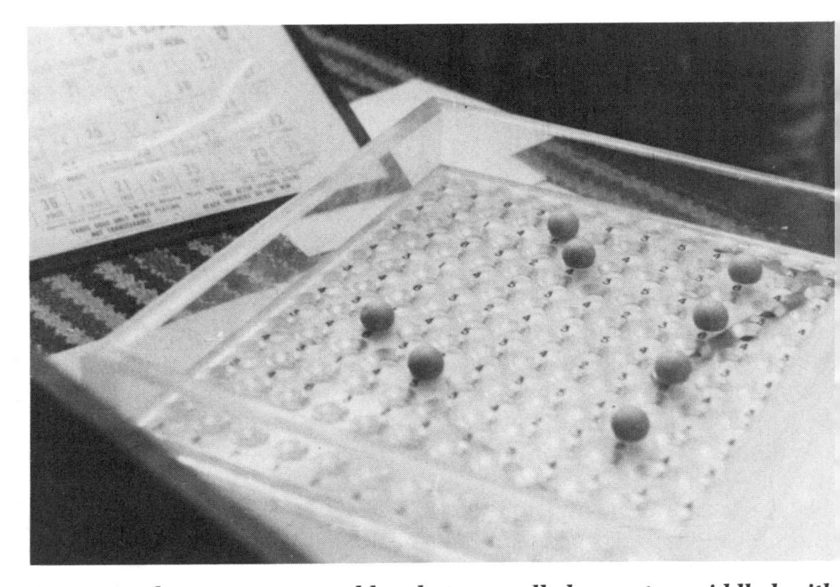

Some Razzle games use marbles that are rolled on a tray riddled with holes bearing numbers. (Photo courtesy of William Riedthaler)

do not question the totals in the early throws of the game, when the operator cheats, or fairbanks, in favor of the player.

The operator lures a person to play by offering a free toss. For instance, the player makes the throw, the operator miscounts and then announces that the player has rolled a 44 – an infrequently occurring number that is worth 50 yards.

The operator states that the prospective player can keep the 50 yards if he or she decides immediately to play. The operator often continues to miscount over the next few turns so the player overcomes the fear of the higher stakes as he or she continues to make good progress toward the 100 yards.

When the stakes are very high, the operator tallies the scores correctly and allows the overwhelming odds against the player to take their toll.

Instead of fast count, Razzles played with pingpong balls or clothespins bearing numbers employ a cheating technique called "peeking." Peeking means the operator obscures one digit of a three-digit number with his or her finger before showing it to the player.

A Razzle using clothespins has the pins standing upright on cords or boards arranged in rows. The player selects from hundreds of pins by circling a pin with a small hoop or rubber jar seal used in home

RAZZLE USING SIX DICE
Expected Occurrence

Number	Frequency	Payoff
8	once in about 1.7 million rolls	100 yards
9	once in 209,952 rolls	100 yards
10	once in 46,656 rolls	50 yards
11	once in 13,997 rolls	30 yards
12	once in 5,090 rolls	50 yards
13	once in 2,121 rolls	50 yards
14	once in 983 rolls	20 yards
15	once in 499 rolls	15 yards
16	once in 273 rolls	10 yards
17	once in 160 rolls	5 yards
18	once in 100 rolls	House Prize
19	once in 66 rolls	House Prize
20	once in 46 rolls	Prize
21	once in 33 rolls	Free Play
22	once in 25 rolls	0 yards
23	once in 20 rolls	0 yards
24	once in 17 rolls	0 yards
25	once in 15 rolls	0 yards
26	once in 13 rolls	0 yards
27	once in 13 rolls	0 yards
28	once in 12 rolls	0 yards
29	once in 13 rolls	Pay Double
30	once in 13 rolls	0 yards
31	once in 15 rolls	0 yards
32	once in 17 rolls	0 yards
33	once in 20 rolls	0 yards
34	once in 25 rolls	Bonus
35	once in 33 rolls	Free Play
36	once in 46 rolls	Prize
37	once in 66 rolls	House Prize
38	once in 100 rolls	House Prize
39	once in 160 rolls	2 yards
40	once in 273 rolls	5 yards
41	once in 499 rolls	15 yards
42	once in 983 rolls	20 yards
43	once in 2,121 rolls	50 yards
44	once in 5,090 rolls	50 yards
45	once in 13,997 rolls	30 yards
46	once in 46,656 rolls	50 yards
47	once in 209,952 rolls	100 yards
48	once in about 1.7 million	100 yards

Source: FBI Law Enforcement Bulletin

In a Pin Store, players encircle clothespins with rubber canning rings. Each clothespin bears a number (above). Carnies can control the outcome of the game by obscuring part of the number with their thumb. (Photo courtesy of William Riedthaler)

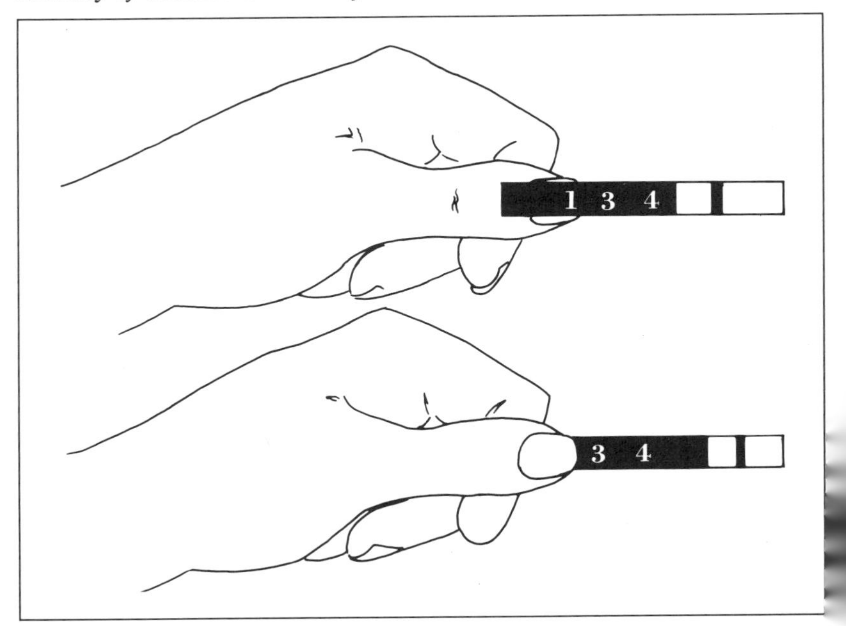

canning. Each pin theoretically bears a two- or three-digit number.

Generally, two-digit numbers between 21 and 41 are winners, and three-digit numbers from 121 to 141 are losers. There may not be any winning yardage or mileage pins on the board.

To cheat in favor of the player, the operator will place his or her thumb over the first spot of a three-digit number. For instance, the operator can change 138, which is worth nothing, into 38, which is worth 50 miles or yards.

Operators also may thrust the pin quickly toward the player's face and miscall the number, and the player accepts the operator's word without discerning the correct number.

Blower Ball, a Razzle frequently found on the midway, uses perhaps 500 pingpong balls bearing two- and three-digit numbers similar to the clothespin game. Operators of Blower Ball employ peeking and miscalled numbers to manipulate the game.

Chapter 35

Scissor Bucket Over the Rail

Scissor Bucket and Over the Rail are frauds, pure and simple. Don't play them, and do others a favor by advising them not to play these rigged games. They cannot be operated in a legitimate manner because they employ a mechanical device hidden from the player.

Players who see such a game operating on a midway, or in another location such as a highway rest stop, should report the activity to police immediately. Only grifters operate Scissor Bucket and Over the Rail games.

Although a Scissor Bucket does not resemble an Over the Rail game, the two are similar in the way they are gaffed. Both employ a drumhead-like bottom and a hidden mechanical damper that deadens the bounce of a ball.

Scissor Bucket

The object of Scissor Bucket – called Chinese Basketball when the bucket is in the shape of a hexagon – is to rebound a hard-rubber or wooden ball off the bottom of an angled bucket, so that the ball falls through a hole in the side of the bucket.

The player must do this successfully three or more times to win.

As might be expected, the player accomplishes the first and second throws with ease. But the ball takes a more powerful rebound on the third toss and flies over the lip of the bucket without traveling through the hole.

The reason for the losing throw is that the spring in the bucket's

Scissors Bucket is a gaffed game that no one should play.

bottom has been altered without the player's knowledge. The bottom of the bucket is made of a thin board instead of the relatively thick boards that make up the sides of the bucket.

Carnival investigator Riedthaler says that a Scissor Bucket he examined had a 1/8-inch-thick birch board in place of the original 3/4-inch-thick plywood board that served as the bucket's bottom.

Behind the game, and hidden from the player, is a see-saw type mechanism running from the bucket down to the pocket that catches the ball after it falls (see diagram).

On one end of the see-saw is a wooden disc that fits against the bottom of the bucket. When it rests against the bucket bottom, the disc dampens the bounce of the ball. On the other end of the see-saw is a rectangular board that is struck by the ball after it falls through the hole.

The operator sets the damper against the bucket bottom to begin the game. The player tosses the ball against the bottom, and the damper absorbs most of the ball's energy and flies back. The deadened ball then falls through the hole and strikes the other end of the see-saw, which resets the damper on the bottom of the bucket.

Since the game resets itself, the carny simply retrieves the ball from the pocket and hands it to the player for the next toss.

After the player makes two successful throws, the operator says something like: "Only one more to make for the big prize," and raps the ball against the bottom of the bucket before handing it over.

That rap knocks the damper away from the bucket bottom. When the player tosses the ball, it rebounds over the lip of the bucket be-

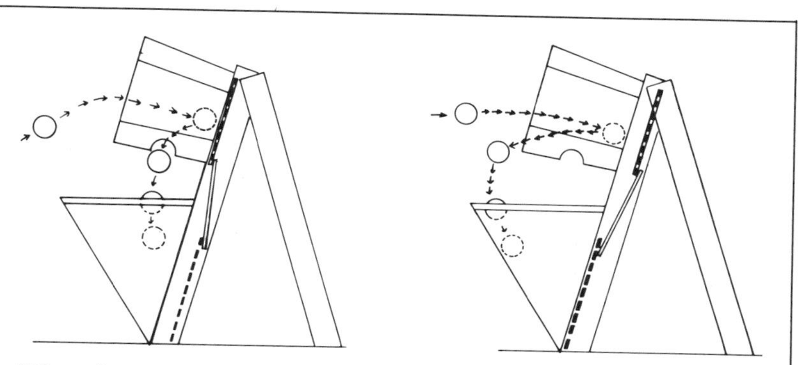

When damper is against bucket bottom, the ball falls through hole (left). When damper is away from bucket bottom, the ball rebounds out of the bucket (right).

cause the bottom now acts with the spring of a drumhead.

Riedthaler says that a carny also can cause a player to lose by catching the ball after it falls through the hole on the second toss and before it strikes the other end of the damper. In that case, the damper has not been reset.

Over the Rail

Over the Rail also employs a secret damping device that resets itself.

The object of Over the Rail is to roll a ball the size of a pool cue ball down a short inclined ramp so that it strikes the front half of a rectangular wooden box, rebounds over a divider in the middle of the box, and lands in the back half.

As with Scissor Bucket, the player finds he or she can accomplish this twice but never the third time for a win.

In Over the Rail, the see-saw runs underneath the length of the box. The damper lies beneath the bottom of the front half of the box, and the other end of the see-saw lies under the back half of the box. The box usually is lined with a heavy cloth so any disturbance in the bottom can't be detected by the player.

To begin the game, the operator sets the damper so it does not rest against the bottom of the front half. The ball rolls down the incline, rebounds against the springy bottom, and flies over the divider. However, the carny catches the ball before it lands in the back half of the box.

As long as the operator catches the ball before it strikes the box's back half, the ball will continue to hurdle the divider.

To make the player lose, the carny merely allows the ball to land. The damper then is pushed against the bottom of the box's front half. On the next roll, the damper will absorb much of the ball's energy, and the ball will fail to fly over the divider.

Like Scissor Bucket, Over the Rail uses a hidden damper to cheat the player.

Chapter 36

Six Cat

Six Cat, also called Turnaround Tom or Big Tom by carnies, was a fixture on the midway until law enforcement agents began cracking down on gaffed games in the '60s and '70s. The game can still be found in a few small ragtag outfits, but only occasionally.

Simply put, don't play Six Cat or Big Tom. They are, by definition, gaffed games where the player wins only if the carny allows it – which rarely happens.

These games should not be confused with Cat Rack, a legitimately run game that is described earlier in this book. A Cat Rack uses as many as 100 small stuffed targets, while Six Cat gets its name because there are only six, relatively large targets.

The lure of Six Cat or Big Tom is the size of the target and the distance at which one throws a baseball; to the player, it seems a sure thing to be able to knock such a large cat off the shelf and win.

The targets are a handful of stuffed cats 18 to 20 inches tall standing on a shelf at the rear of the joint. The cats rest at a height of about 5½ feet, and a strip of wood or slat running along the front of the shelf protects their bases from being hit. The player makes his throw with a baseball from a distance of about eight feet.

The Secret

Carnival consultant Snyder says the trick is that "the cats are so close, it seems almost impossible that they can't be knocked over."

The object of the game is to hit three cats out of three shots so that

This diagram illustrates a simple method that carnies have used for decades to gaff a Six Cat. To make sure the cat cannot be knocked off its stand, the carny sets the cat up against a front peg. The cat will not fall because its center of gravity is behind the back edge of the stand.

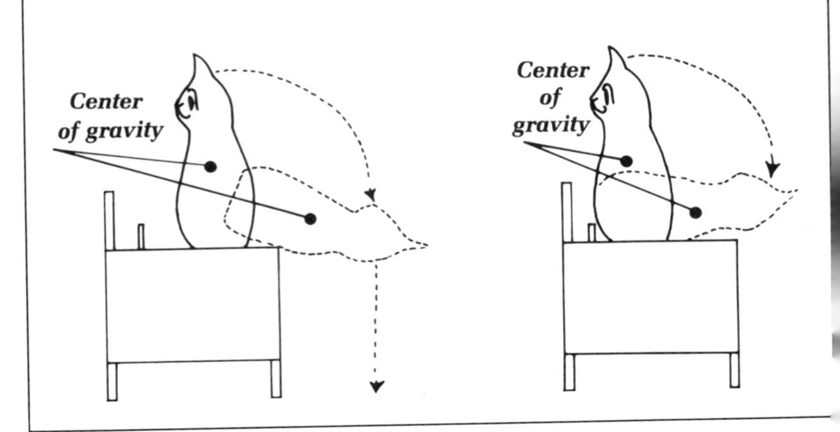

they fall completely off the shelf. The strategy is to hit them dead center, throwing the ball as hard as possible.

Operators gaff the games so the players knock the first two cats off the shelves, but are unable to accomplish this with a third cat.

There are several ways operators can rig the game.

The simplest gaff is that some of the cats are weighted so heavily they cannot be knocked off the shelf. A.K. Brill, in his directions to carnies on how to build a Six Cat game, advises that "some operators weight four cats with flat irons, so two can be knocked off, but it takes real skill to knock off three."

"However," Brill writes, "as it takes winners to make your game popular, weighting two would be more logical."

Other carnies make a gripper at the rear of the cat's base by driving several nails into the shelf so their tips protrude about one-half inch through the wood. When the cat falls backwards, the protruding nails catch its base or fabric.

A Turnaround Tom game gets its name from the special type of two-faced cats that can be upset only if the correct side is facing the player, Snyder says. Each cat has a wooden base a few inches wide, 7 inches long, and about as thick as a 2-by-4. The cat is attached close to the front of the rectangular wood base.

If the short edge of the base is facing the player, the game is nearly impossible to win because the impact of the ball must overcome the ledge of wood behind the cat, as well as the cat itself. But if the cat is turned around, it is fairly easy to knock off the shelf because the base no longer acts as leverage against the player.

The now-defunct Evans-Oakes Co. in Chicago made a game that worked on this principle, only it used one cat that was set atop a suitcase.

A variation on this gaff is that the front base of the cat is beveled so it fits into a groove along the slat where it meets the shelf. This allows the cat to be knocked down, but not off, as the lip of the bevel absorbs much of the ball's force.

Carnival investigator Riedthaler says some carnies rig Big Tom through use of a "thumb gaff," so-called because the carny uses his thumb to gauge a distance at which the cat is placed from the front of the shelf so the game cannot be won.

If a carny wants to set the game so a player can win, he puts the cat's base snug against the front of the shelf. When the cat it struck, it will fall off because it can slip between the back edge of the shelf and a rail directly behind the shelf.

But if the carny sets the cat's base with a thumb's distance from the front slat, the player cannot win because the cat's head bridges the distance between the shelf and the rear rail.

Riedthaler says some carnies gaff a Six Cat game by using a "rocker and cradle." By means of a secret control, the carny can move a rear rail out far enough so it will hold up the cat's head when the stuffed animal is knocked over. Consequently, the player loses because the cat has not fallen off the shelf.

Some agents use a foot pedal to control the rail. Others set their Six Cats next to other joints so the gaff can be operated by the agents – called "gunners" – next door. The grifter usually gives a voice signal, such as stating a phrase to the player, that tips off the confederate next door to open or close the rail.

Chapter 37

Swinger

There is a whole family of games that seem to depend upon the skill of a player to knock over a pin or tall object by using a ball as a pendulum.

But, while it looks like a game of skill, Swinger, or Aerial Bowling, is a rigged game that suckers have lost thousands of dollars playing. Stay away from a Swinger if you see it on a midway.

These are favorite games of grifters, who will allow a player to win "practice" games until the game is played for real.

A typical Swinger game uses a small hard ball that is suspended by a chain connected to a frame. The ball is about 5 inches in diameter, the chain about 3 feet long. A 15-inch bowling pin is placed on the spot directly beneath the ball.

Other games use a baseball and a wooden cone, a small bowling ball and a tall prize such as a carton of cigarettes, a ball and two pins, or a ball and a soft-drink bottle. Regardless of the equipment used, the principles of rigging the game are the same.

The Secret

The object of the game is to swing the ball past the pin and knock it over on the return shot. If the pin is placed exactly plumb of the ball, the game is impossible to win.

Physics tells us that the ball will make its return swing at the same distance from the pin as it its forward swing. So if the ball clears the pin on the front swing – which is a basic rule of the game – it will

Swinger is a game players can win only if they defy the laws of physics.

pass by the pin on the back swing.

The agent wants people to play, however, so he often gives players practice swings to encourage them to lay down their money, and sets the game so they will win. There are three ways an agent can allow a player to win: by setting the pin so it doesn't rest immediately below the ball, by moving the frame that supports the ball, or by using sleight of hand to knock the pin over for the player.

Law enforcement agencies report that pins on these games sometimes have a small slot carved in their bottoms. The slot fits over a small nail protruding from the base of the game. When an agent wants a player to win, he simply shoves the pin to one side of the slot so the whole pin is offset from plumb. All the agent has to do to make the game impossible to beat is slide the pin to the other side of the slot.

Other agents use their little finger to measure a space between the pin and a wooden crotch that sets the pin in plumb. When they want the player to lose, agents push the pin tight in the crotch.

In an older method of rigging the game, agents always put the pin in the same spot, but they would move the frame from which the ball hangs so that players would win. The frame is centered when the agent wants a player to lose.

Another method of cheating employs sleight of hand called a duke shot, where the agent shortens the arc of the ball during its return swing so it knocks the pin down.

In the game of Aerial Bowling, carnivalgoers play for very large stuffed animals or portable stereos. Players can win the grand prize by accomplishing 10 strikes in a row, and they must pay for each frame of the bowling game. Agents will allow players to win nine frames, but will see that they lose on the 10th frame – and miss the grand prize.

Chapter 38

Pokerino

Pokerino falls into that category of game a skilled carny can win with ease, but for the average person, winning is largely a matter of luck.

The game combines the elements of a slot machine and a 50-card playing deck, which can be minus the deuce and trey of diamonds. The object of Pokerino is to draw the best poker hand by pushing five buttons that freeze drums spinning inside the machine. On each of the drums are the faces of 10 cards, distributed in random fashion.

The better the poker hand, the better the prize. Usually, the player accumulates coupons for larger prizes, as the agent gives out slum for only a few coupons.

The Secret

Although Pokerino agents have demonstrated that it is possible to draw high-ranking hands at will on the machines, it is a matter of luck when an average player draws a good hand. In general, the odds of the average player drawing a high-ranking hand depend on which drums are inserted in the machine.

Some machines may offer only 10 different cards on the five drums. So, while it would be possible to draw five of a kind, it would not be possible to draw a royal flush.

A study conducted by the Michigan attorney general's office concluded that the drums spin too fast for the average person to freeze at will a specific moving card seen through the clear plastic window of

Pokerino is a game of chance for the average carnivalgoer, law enforcement agents say.

the machine.

Further, the study indicated that it would take the average player hours to learn the position of all the cards on a machine.

In Pokerino, an electric motor spins a shaft upon which the five drums are mounted. A Teflon sleeve with a diameter slightly larger than the axle is fitted inside the hub of each drum. There is a clamp around each sleeve, tightened to the point that friction turns the drum with the spinning shaft. There also are 10 pegs on the hub of the drum.

When a player presses the stop button, a solenoid inside the machine forces a brake between the pegs – freezing the card shown on the face of the drum. The last drums to be stopped turn slightly more slowly than normal because of drag created on the shaft by drums frozen earlier.

The attorney general's study of five machines showed that the drums moved at an average rate of about 61 revolutions per minute. Since there are 10 cards mounted on the circumference of the wheel, the player would see a card for about one-tenth of a second.

According to studies of highway driving, it takes about two-tenths of a second for an alert young adult to recognize something visually. And an alert person also needs slightly more than a half second to push a button after recognizing a visual signal, the attorney general's office says.

In addition, investigators found that it could take up to .125 seconds from the time the button is pushed until the brake stops the drum from spinning. The average delay time was about .045 seconds for three machines that were tested.

Assuming an alert carnivalgoer is playing an average Pokerino game, it would take almost three-quarters of a second from the time a card is sighted to the time the drum is stopped. So the player essentially would be "drawing" a card perhaps seven cards after the one he desired.

Theoretically, a person could still draw a good hand if he knew the location of all the cards. Of four machines examined, all used only five types of drums.

Investigators found that one machine used five identical drums, with four drums showing cards in the same order. The fifth drum was simply turned over before being inserted on the axle, so that the order of the cards was reversed.

Glossary of Terms

advance man – employee who handles details such as licenses and sponsors before a carnival arrives in town; sometimes used to describe an employee who handles bribes.

add-up joint – game where points are totaled for the player.

agent – employee of the concession operator.

alibi agents – agents who refuse to give a prize to a player who won legitimately on the grounds of an alibi, such as leaning over the foul line, etc.

arcade – a tent housing coin-operated amusement games.

back end – the rear of the midway that has rides and shows.

bag man – the person to whom bribes are paid.

bally – a free show held to attract an audience; the front of a concession.

barker – agent of a show who gives a spiel.

bat away – take players' money as quickly as possible in a gaffed game, usually when it is known that police won't interfere.

bean – amphetamines.

blank – engagement that hasn't paid off; player with only a few dollars.

bloomer – an engagement with poor business.

blowoff – collect another admission to a special attraction of a show after the audience is seated.

booth – game run by a community group or sponsor, rather than by professional carnies.

boost – stolen goods.
Bozo – clown character who insults patrons so they will try to throw baseballs at a target and drop him into a dunk tank.
build up – excite a player into gambling further.
burn the lot – when a carnival owner allows agents to cheat because he has no intention of returning to the location hosting the carnival.
broad tosser – operator of a three-card monte game.
call – opening time of a carnival.
cake-eaters – players, usually in a rural area.
center joint – concession placed in the middle of the midway that can handle players from all four sides.
chump – naive player.
circus candy – cheap candy contained in an impressive-looking box.
committee – sponsor of a carnival.
concessions – the foods stands, games and shops on a midway.
cookhouse – place where carnies eat that is generally not open to the public.
count stores – gaffed games where numbers are added up to determine whether a player wins.
cut in – expense of getting electricity.
cradle – pedal or handle that controls a rigged game.
ding – operator's expenses such as utilities and trash collection.
donniker – toilet.
ducat – token that gives a player free admission to game or show.
duke – when an accomplice working for the agent persuades someone to play.
duke shot – illegal shot taken by the operator of a Swinger game to prove that the game can be won.
fairbank – to do something for a player so that he thinks he has gained an advantage, such as losing a small amount of money, giving an extra ball, miscounting in the player's favor, etc.
fast count – when the carny tallies a score swiftly so the player cannot confirm the result.
feature – a game that an agent operates especially well.
fence-to-fence operation – one where the carnival owner controls who can set up a concession on the midway.
fix – bribe.
fixer – carnival employee who handles payoffs to local police and complaints about rigged games.
flash – prizes on display; the appearance of the prizes.

flat stores – games set up solely for the purpose of cheating players as quickly as possible.

flattie – agent of a flat store, usually a sophisticated carny.

floater – an operator who travels from one carnival to another.

floss – cotton candy.

forty-milers – small carnivals that don't travel far from home base; a rookie carny.

front end – the place on the midway that has games.

fuzz – police.

G-top – a private club at the carnival where operators can drink and gamble.

G-wheel – rigged wheel of fortune.

gaff – rig a game so a player cannot win.

gig – take all of a player's money in one try.

gillies, gilly outfit – small carnivals that usually travel the rural circuit.

go wrong – when an agent loses money.

grab-stands, grab-joints – food outlets on the midway that are run by carnies.

grifter – agent of a joint that can be worked honestly or strong.

grind show – show where there is a continuous spiel to attract players.

grind stores – synonymous with flat stores.

gunner – confederate who helps run a Six Cat.

handle – how a game is rigged.

hanky panks – a game where it is guaranteed that a player wins a prize.

heat – police; dissatisfied customers causing problems.

Hey Rube – a call for help when carnies are in trouble with outsiders.

ice – bribes to allow illegal games to operate.

Ikey Heyman – a rigged wheel of fortune that employs a friction brake on the axle so the wheel can be stopped wherever the agent wants.

independents – operators who have rented footage on the midway, but are not associated with the carnival.

inside man – concessionaire who employs an outside man to operate a game.

jam auction – a show on the midway where inferior goods are sold under the subterfuge that the auctioneer works for the products' manufacturers.

jenny – merry-go-round.

joing – rigging a game so it cannot be won.

joint – a carnival midway concession.

jointee – concession operator.
juice – bribes paid to police.
jump – move between engagements.
key girl – a ruse where an agent sells keys to the room of a woman working in the carnival to players who believe she will dispense favors.
kootch – strip-tease dancers.
lay down – board upon which players place their bets.
laying it down – when the agent describes how the game is played.
left-hand side – when entering through the main ticket booth, the left side is considered a poorer location for concessions than the right side.
live one – player who has money.
lot – the site of the carnival.
lot lice – carnivalgoers who browse and spend nothing.
lousy, losum game – when an operator tells an agent to immediately stop the game, usually if the operator suspects the player will complain.
marks – players.
mender – patch or lawyer who travels with the carnival.
mitt camp – palm readers.
midway – combined attractions of the carnival.
money store – games that pay players in cash.
mooch – player.
mug joint – concession that sells souvenir photos to players.
nut – rent paid to carnival owner.
orders – restrictions set on the operators by the carnival owner.
outside man – accomplice.
outsider – a person not associated with the carnival or carnival life.
paper – posters or advertisements for a carnival.
patch – a carnival employee who acts as liaison between the carnival and the police; a carnival general manager.
patch money – money paid by operators to keep the police away.
peek store – gaffed game where the operator can change the outcome by obscuring part of a number with a finger – for instance, changing 138 to 38 by placing a finger over the 1.
peek the poke – when an agent employs an accomplice to observe players with money so they can be conned.
percentage games, PCs – games where the operator takes a set percentage, usually games of chance.
piece – an item of stock.

plaster – cheap prizes made of plaster that appear more valuable than they are; any type of cheap prize.
play – engagement.
plush – stuffed animals.
privilege – rent paid to operate on the midway.
punks – small stuffed animals on a rack; dolls; children.
racket – any operation that depends on deception for success.
racket show – carnival that derives most of its revenues from rigged games.
ragtags – small carnivals that travel the rural circuits; tattered shows.
rail show – carnival that travels on its own train.
reader – a phony driver's license.
red one – a profitable engagement.
ride monkey – carnival employee who operates the rides.
right-hand side – when entering through the main ticket booth of the midway, the right side is considered a better location than the left side for concessions.
roughies – temporary help hired to erect or pack a carnival.
route – a season's engagements of the carnival.
scuffling – low point in the year when there is no work and money is tight.
sharpers, sharpies – players who have practiced a carnival game to the point where they can win easily.
shill – accomplices working for an agent who are allowed to "win" prizes to falsely demonstrate how easily a game can be beaten.
skill games – games where players with ability have a good chance to win.
slough – pack up tent and equipment for the next engagement.
slum – prizes worth only pennies.
sticks – confederates who pose as players but work for the agent. Sometimes, sticks persuade a player to join them in a conspiracy against the agent, only to cheat the player of his money.
stick joint – a portable concession fashioned from rough lumber and canvas.
still dates – engagements that have a history, but aren't connected with a fair.
stock – general term for prize merchandise.
stores – concessions that are rigged.
strong – cheating at a fair game that can be rigged; a girlie show that is liberal.
tear down – pack up for the next engagement.

ten-in-one – sideshow or freak show.
tip – game players or audience at a show.
townie – local help hired by a carny to help set up and tear down.
trailer joint – a concession housed in a trailer that is towed to the site of a carnival.
truck show – a carnival that moves by truck.
two-way joint – a game that can be converted in seconds from one that is played fairly to one that is rigged.
tub – the seat of a ride.
"with it" – a phrase that means one is a carny.

Bibliography

Works of reference consulted by the author in preparation of this book are:

FOX, THERON. How to make Money with Carnival Games. Atlanta, Ga.: The Pinchpenny Press, 1980.

GIBSON, WALTER B. Carnival Gaffs. Las Vegas, Nev.: Gambler's Book Club Press, 1976.

QUINN, JOHN PHLIP. Gambling and Gambling Devices. Las Vegas, Nev.: Gambler's Book Club Press, 1912.

RIEDTHALER, WILLIAM. Carnival Games, Gambling and Frauds. Tallahassee, Fla.: Florida Department of Law Enforcement, 1987.

SCARNE, JOHN. Scarne's Complete Guide to Gambling. New York, N.Y.: Simon and Schuster, 1961.

SORROWS, GENE. All About Carnivals. Miami, Fla.: American Federation of Police, 1985.

Index

Order Form

Zenith Press
P.O. Box 248
Royal Oak, Michigan
48068

Please send me the following:

______ copies of Carnival Secrets at $14.95, softcover $______.___

Michigan residents add 4 percent sales tax ______.___

Shipping: $1.25 for first book,
50 cents each additional book ______.___

Total order $______.___

Name: ______________________________

Address: ______________________________

______________________________ Zip Code: __________

I understand that I may return the book for a full refund within 10 days if not satisfied.

EAU CLAIRE DISTRICT LIBRARY